IF YOU HAVE GOD YOU HAVE EVERYTHING

A FAITH ADVENTURE OF A YOUNG BULGARIAN WOMAN

DEDICATION

This book is dedicated to my Savior and best friend Jesus,
who has always been there for me in the good times and in the
tough times. His love and faithfulness have helped me live on.
I also dedicate this book to all those who dare to dream big
and to those who move beyond their natural abilities;
to the ones who are brave and take risks.

CONTENTS

COMMENTS

IF YOU HAVE GOD YOU HAVE EVERYTHING

"WOW! What a book! "If You Have God You Have Everything" is a great testimony to the powerful hand of God on Ceitci's life. Her faith in God and desire to please Him is a great inspiration. The second edition is currently being lived out! I highly recommend this book to anyone who wants to leave the lowlands of complacency and mediocrity and ascend the heights of destiny! **It will challenge you to boldly go where you have never gone before in your walk with Him!**"

Bill Meyer
Founder and Director, Reach Now International – Tulsa, OK

"This book will encourage and stir your faith to press beyond the boundaries you see with your natural eyes. It will challenge you to move into the "exceeding abundantly" realm that many people never achieve and then will cause you to reach your destiny. **A true story of true faith in action!**"

Phil Stern
Founder and Director, Feed the Forgotten – St. Louis, MO

"Look what the Lord has done! Ceitci Demirkova has been a refreshing part of our lives since 1994. We met this young woman while on a short term mission's trip to Bulgaria. Over the years we have watched the reality of this book come to pass in her life. **As you read, "If You Have God You Have Everything." you will be challenged and encouraged to live and walk by faith.** This book will be an inspiration to both young believers and mature Christians!"

Jim and Stacy Raymond
Senior Pastors, Verdigris Valley Christian Center – Altoona, KS

"From the first day I met Ceitci, I knew the hand of the Lord was on her. She responded so quickly to the Gospel message, and it was obvious the Lord would use her for His glory. **I am sure that everyone reading this book will be challenged to serve the Lord more than ever before.** The Lord has done great things for Ceitci, and she has a simple but strong way to say things. Her testimony is true. If you have God, you have everything you need. He is all we need. I am a friend and coworker with this dear woman of God."

Paul Stern
Founding Director, Encouragers Unlimited Ministries

"In this book Ceitci builds on one of God's promises. All things really do work together for the good of those who love Him. This book is *'must read'* material for those desiring to understand God's will and God's ways."

Randy Downing
Senior Pastor, The Rock Church - Danville, IL

ACKNOWLEDGEMENTS

Ceitci would like to give special
acknowledgements and thanks to:

IF YOU HAVE GOD YOU HAVE EVERYTHING

My wonderful parents, Angel and Slavka Demirkovi: Because of you I am here today! How could I begin to thank you for your unconditional and sacrificial love you've shown me over the years! You always believed in me and gave me the best! I am proud to have you as my parents! You are my greatest example of people who walk in humility and are willing to lay down their life for others! You mean more to me than any words can express! I love you with my whole heart!

My grandmother, Mitka: You are awesome! Thanks for all the wonderful meals you prepared for me while growing up! You were the only one who was willing to put up with me everyday after I came home from school. I will forever cherish all the fun memories! I love you, Grandma!

Jim and Stacy Raymond: Wow, who could have ever imagined that one short-term mission's trip to my country, would make you a part of my life forever! You were my first family here in the United States! Thank you for your love and for always being there for me! I love you!

Paul and Eleanor Stern: Your life is an encouragement and inspiration to me! Thank you for your heart and love for the nations that motivated you to come to Bulgaria and bring to us the good news of the Gospel! I love you!

Shirley Martin: I still remember the day in the Mission's office when I said that I was looking for a family to live with. Without a hesitation you took me in. Thank you for opening your home to me and accepting me as I am. We've had some wonderful years together. You are very special to me and have blessed me in more ways than can be expressed! Thank you also for helping me with the book and making it a reality! I love you!

Pastors Billy Joe and Sharon Daugherty: I will forever cherish the years I had in Tulsa, OK, and the privilege to be underneath your ministry. By living out the Gospel before us, you've helped me to see the Father's heart. Praying for the nations and winning souls for the Lord is why we are here. While being a part of Victory Christian Center, my vision was expended to reach the nations and my faith was strengthened. Thank you for your love and dedication!

Ron McIntosh: You were one of the first people who ignited the fire in me to see revival spread across the nations. Thank you for being a great VBI director, who believed in your students and always encouraged us to go further in the Lord! I appreciate your obedience to the Lord!

Dr. T.L. Osborn: You and Dr. Daisy have inspired me, and many others to preach the Gospel with simplicity and power. Thank you for your dedication to the Lord and for your heart for the nations of the world. By seeing your examples and reading your books God has stirred a passion in me to never stop ministering Jesus to others! I am forever grateful for your lives!

Dr. LaDonna Osborn: I count it a special privilege to personally know you and learn from you. You are one of my greatest examples of a woman, who is highly devoted to the Lord and therefore is used by Him to touch and transform nations! Thank you for setting a standard for all of us women in ministry! Thank you also for being a part of this book! I love you!

Charlie and Verda Wheeler (and the whole family): This is one of those divine appointments, when God placed us in each other's lives! You were not only my housing directors, you were my family! Thank you for loving me so much, for encouraging me and for making me a part of your lives! I love you all!

Colleen Judd: You were one of the first people, who believed in me and the call of God on my life! Thank you for your obedience to the Lord, for your love and support throughout the years! I love you!

Bill and Leslie Meyer: You were the greatest directors I've ever had! Only nine months in the IMT program, but my life was impacted forever! You've taught me that people are more important than programs, and sharing Jesus with others is what our life goal should be! Thank you for being examples and true leaders! I love you!

Laurie and Preston Hobart: What an incredible way for us to meet a few years back. That in itself is a testimony of God's predestined plan for our lives. He knew how much I needed you in my life! You have been like 'a mom and a dad' to me. You have proven that I can always count on you for many things! Thank you for being there to listen, laugh and cry with me! You are a great example and an encouragement! I love you!

John O'Hara: thank you for being so obedient to the Lord that one day in VBI. I had a need and God supplied it through you!!! I appreciate you and your family and value our friendship! I love you all!

Heidi Ruotolo: From roommates in Bible School, to close as sisters, to best friends, you are forever in my heart! God knew I needed someone as wild as me, who would look at the world through the eyes of faith and enjoy even the most simple moments of life! Thank you for being there for me and for introducing me to the great Northwest, especially Seattle, WA! Also, thank you for sharing your family with me! I love you girl!

All my Aloha friends in Seattle, WA: You have shown me the true meaning of being friends in a covenant relationship! Thank you for standing in the gap for me, for always encouraging me and cheering me on, for supporting me and accepting me for who I am! I love you all!

Mark and Joani Akers: What a plan God had! He brought me all the way to St. Louis and placed me in your home. The first day we met I felt like we had known each other all of our lives. Your love for people and for the nations is expressed through the compassion I see in you daily. Thank you for making me a part of your lives and family! Thank you for all your help with this book! I love you!

Kent Henry: Thank you for being so real and passionately in love with the Lord. You truly lead us into the throne room of God, where we bow our hearts in adoration before Him! God has always ministered to me through your prophetic songs and has brought freedom and encouragement into my heart! I'm honored to know you!

Gospel Media Publishing Company (Joel Sjoberg): Spreading the Gospel, by being on fire and passionately pursing God is a great example and inspiration to many others and me. Thank you for being one of my 'forerunners', who showed me that even if we are young we still have something to write about, a testimony to tell!

I am privileged to have my first book published at your company! Thank you!

All my supporters, friends and people who have been a part of this book becoming reality: Even though I can't mention all of your names on this page, your sacrifice and encouragement will never be forgotten. Thank you for your letters, e-mails and phone calls showing me how much you care! We are all world changers for God's glory! I love you all!

FOREWORD

by Dr. LaDonna Osborn

The mysteries that lay hidden behind the Communist curtains of Eastern Europe and the greater Eurasia caused fear and anxiety among many Westerners, even Christians, for decades. But as these government systems have collapsed the real life stories of women and men have begun to emerge. We are now becoming awakened to the reality of God's great love reaching and touching people in ways that only He could orchestrate. When some thought these nations were beyond hope, God's Spirit was at work.

If You Have God You Have Everything is a testimony to God's determined will to reconcile people to Himself and then to live through them to likewise reconcile others. Ceitci Demirkova is a living witness to God's grace that redeems people who believe on Christ, and to God's Spirit who restores people to His eternal purpose. Ceitci is sharing her own story through this book as a reminder that with God, all things are possible.

IF YOU HAVE GOD YOU HAVE EVERYTHING

During my lifetime of ministry in scores of nations I have personally witnessed tens of thousands of miracle wonders of God. The blind receiving sight, the lepers being cleansed, the deaf and crippled being restored to health and vitality are awesome miracles. Yet the greatest miracle occurs when a person is reconnected with God through the wonder of the new birth.

Regardless of nationality, language, culture, religious tradition, or any other distinctive, people everywhere are hopeless unless they know God through Jesus Christ. Wherever we proclaim the Gospel with clarity and with evidence of Christ's life people receive Him gladly. His love-power then transforms the most broken life into one of dignity and true purpose. This is what happened to Ceitci. It is a miracle and it must be told.

As you read this *faith adventure of a young Bulgarian woman,* your faith will be stirred to believe God in the midst of your own impossibilities. Allow this story to impact your life. When God was at work rescuing Ceitci, He foreknew that you would one day hold her testimony in your hands. He talked to her; He is now talking to you. You may feel, as Ceitci did at times in her life, that you have nothing to offer. But the reality is, *if you have God, you have everything!*

LaDonna C. Osborn, D.Min.

INTRODUCTION

It was a cold winter's day in November 1994 and just a few days after a really bad snowstorm. The freezing breeze went through every bone of my body as I walked quickly and pressed against the wind. Finally I made it over the hill and entered the warm house where my friend, Stella, and her family were gathered to have praise, worship and seek God for direction. We were living in times of change and desperation. Bulgaria was going through economical and spiritual turmoil, which began after the fall of the Communist regime. All economic dependency on the government was discarded for capitalist and open markets. And the state-run church, Greek Orthodox, started to rise up in power and influence. The combination of these caused confusion and instability for the Bulgarian people.

I didn't know about the vision that would be planted in my heart that night. A vision you will read about in the chapters of this book.

Little did I know that two weeks later I would be getting on a plane and flying to the USA where I had been accepted to attend Victory Bible Institute in Tulsa, Oklahoma. Many thoughts rushed through my mind. I had thoughts of fear but also thoughts of comfort. I knew that in spite of what would take place, God would not leave me to face it alone. A picture right above the couch where I was sitting had the following quote written on it, "When God is all you have, you will understand that the Lord is all you need." Below the quote it said, "Author unknown." It has been several years since I read that, but the quote remains with me. When I went home that night I wrote the quote in my journal but it seems like God wrote it in my heart. Through the years it has become a theme in my life. In every situation or in whatever circumstance I found myself in, I would always say, "If I have God, I have everything." That is the theme of this book you are holding in your hands. God has placed an abundance of potential inside of each one of us. As we live for Him, He reveals to us His purpose and calling for our lives.

> When God is all you have, you will understand that the Lord is all you need.

GOD WANTS TO USE YOU

Many people look at themselves and regret the fact that they were born on this earth. Others try to accomplish everything by only relying on their own abilities, knowledge or material possessions.[1] My desire for you as a reader is that you will be inspired and challenged by the Lord while reading this book. He longs to perform miracles for us and through us. The requirement left for you and me is to believe that what He said in the Bible is the truth and can take place today in our life.

God is not afraid of using you even if you have insecurities and He is not shocked when you fail the first time in trying to obey His voice. I pray the stories shared here will open your eyes to see it's your availability, not abilities, that matter to God. My life is a testimony to that. The stories of my days in Bulgaria, the lifestyle I had during the Communist regime, and the way God transformed me, all testify that God is able, and with Him all things become possible.

When God placed a burden on my heart to share these testimonies by compiling them in a book, my natural mind resisted. I have never written a book before and I had to write in English, which is my second language. As I looked through my journals I had accumulated over the past years and as I read through the testimonies of the miracles God had done in my short lifetime, my mind was overwhelmed, but my spirit was soaring. From my experience, when we attempt to do what is impossible, God steps in and provides for all of our needs.

WITH GOD ALL THINGS ARE POSSIBLE

One of my favorite verses in the Bible is found in Luke 1:37. It says, *"For with God all things are possible."* Chapter one of Luke talks about Mary, the mother of Jesus, who had just had a supernatural visitation from the Lord and was informed by an angel that she was pregnant with the Son of God. In her natural mind it didn't make sense, but in the supernatural realm it was already a fact. She only had to believe! When we look up the word 'possible' from that scripture, we find out that it comes from the word "dunatos", which is, "dynamite", "dynasty", "dynamo" and "dynamic." In English it translates "mighty or powerful."[2] It's the same word used in Matthew 19:26, where Jesus was telling the disciples that with men things are impossible but with God all is possible. He is referring to salvation and the ability God has to save a person. What does this leave us with? Basically, the fact that when we have God, He empowers us to do the impossible and to believe the impossible, because it's His dynamite power working in us and enabling us to be all He has called us to be. It is the same power that can snatch you out of the hand of Satan and translate you into the kingdom of God. With God all things are possible, but *we* have to believe and act on that truth. It's up to you and me to step out of the natural and step into the supernatural where God is.

> With God all things are possible, but we have to believe and act on that truth.

My former pastor Billy Joe Daugherty, in Tulsa, OK, used to say, *"When you preach from your mind, you will only touch a mind, but when you preach from your heart, you will touch a heart."* As I share my heart with you, I pray that the Holy Spirit will touch yours and that He will make an eternal difference in your life.

If you only have the Lord you will see that He will become all you need Him to be in every situation. He gives you His favor, His strength, His joy, His power, and His provision. He becomes your Savior, your Daddy, your Best Friend, your Comforter, your Healer, and your Lover. He gives you all you need so that you can accomplish the destiny He has for your life!

Fasten your seatbelt and get ready for an adventure. Remember that, **"If You Have God, You Have Everything."**

Ceitci Demirkova

CHAPTER 1

THE ADVENTURE BEGINS

My heart was pounding and my eyes couldn't believe what I saw through the little window of the plane. Just 12 hours earlier I had been at the airport in Sofia, the capital of Bulgaria, getting ready to walk on to the plane and fly to New York City. It was my first flight and it was my first time to be by myself. I wasn't just going to a different city, but flying to a different country. I guess you could say, it was my 'first' everything. I didn't have time to really think about what was taking place. It was happening so fast! I had to just relax and flow with it. In my heart I had an overwhelming peace.

At that time I did not speak English well. I could understand much more than I could actually speak. Still, it was not enough to understand everything people were saying around me. I now had to communicate with them and be at the right place or I would be lost. Try to put yourself in "my shoes." Imagine that you have just landed in a foreign country where you don't speak the language and you can only understand about every other word of what is being said. I have never written about my flight before, but I can remember almost every single emotion and the different divine appointments with people I had on that day. It was December 5, 1994, a little over three years after I had accepted Jesus as my personal Lord and Savior. Who would have ever thought that a shy girl like me, who could hardly pronounce her name in front of more than two people without fainting, was about to enter into God's destiny for her life. In my mind there was only one question, "God, am I really going to be able to make you proud? Am I capable of carrying the task you have for me?" Considering my insecurity and lack of ability to take care of myself, I realized it would not be me who would make things happen, but God.

As I was having these thoughts rushing through my mind, I heard the flight attendant announce, "In just ten minutes we will be landing in JFK International Airport. Please fasten your seatbelts and bring your seats to an upright position." I looked again through the window. We were flying right above the Statue of Liberty. Because it was night, New York City was alive in lights. It was beautiful. At that moment I really didn't have any words to express how excited and privileged I felt that God had taken control of my life, and He saw more potential in me than I or anyone else had imagined. I was about to enter into a city and country that I had only seen in pictures and movies. Was it a dream or was it reality? I would soon find out.

America had not been my "dream country" where I wanted to live when I grew up. As a matter of fact, I had my own plan and America was not a part of it. In the summer of 1994, I had just graduated from a Language High School in Veliko Turnovo, Bulgaria. I was 18 years of age and my whole life was before me. I had studied four languages: German, Russian, English and Bulgarian. In school I was in a specialized program where I was focused on the German language. For five years I studied the German language and ignored my English classes. So, in spite of the fact that I took English, I had no idea how to speak or read it. It was not on my priority list and I thought English was too hard to learn therefore I didn't even want to try.

Do you wonder why I am starting with these particular stories? I would like you to look into the 'world' from which I came, so you can understand the changes God had to make in my life in order for me to be the person I am today.

GOD PREDESTINES OUR LIVES

I firmly believe that God has a plan for each one of us before we are born into this world. In Jeremiah 1:3, God spoke to Jeremiah when he was still a young man and told him of the plan He had for his life.

> *"Before I formed you in the womb I knew you; before you were born I sanctified you; I ordained you a prophet to the nations."*

This verse speaks of the fact that no one is a mistake and they shouldn't think of themselves as one.[3] It speaks that God predestines our lives. He calls and believes in us, even before we discover His plan. It's comforting to know that God sees the end before the beginning. He already knows all our successes and all our failures yet He still calls us and assigns a mission. Jeremiah felt inadequate and incapable of doing what God had just spoken to him. There is a key in that first chapter and it's found in verses 9 and 10:

> *"Then the Lord put forth His hand and touched my mouth, and the Lord said to me: Behold, I have put My words in your mouth, see, I have this day set you over the nations and over the kingdoms, to root out and to pull down, to destroy and to throw down, to build and to plant."*

It was the Lord who first had the plan. It was God who placed into Jeremiah the abilities He needed in order to become one of the greatest prophets of his time. God touched his mouth and opened his understanding to see the supernatural things He was showing him. That means He placed His anointing on his life and it was God's abilities, not Jeremiah's.

I want you to be set free in the area of trying to do it all by yourself. You simply can't. You can't help God out and you can't outsmart God. Before you were born there was a special call placed by God on your life. You may never be a preacher or a prophet like Jeremiah was, but God has placed unique abilities inside of you that no one ever had or will have. There is something only you can do on this earth. There are people only you can touch. Remember, the key is not figuring out "how, when, and why," but leaning into the purpose of God. All Jeremiah had to do was agree with God. He opened his mouth and the words were already given to him by the Lord. You might not think that it is possible today, but wait. Let me finish the story I started about my German Language School.

> Remember, the key is not figuring out "how, when, and why," but leaning into the purpose of God.

GROWING UP

During the time we were under the Communist regime, our school had a certain system. It didn't matter how intelligent the student was. If they didn't have an inside connection with the teachers or the directors of the school, it was not likely the student would get good grades or be well-respected. I will go into a little bit more detail about that in chapter 2, but what I want you to understand is that the system in those days was not one that took a person's abilities into consideration to bring out their potential. Instead, it made them feel like they were nothing and didn't know anything. Even though I did my homework, every time I was asked to go up to the blackboard and answer the teacher's questions in front of my classmates, my mind would go blank. Sometimes the teachers would see how nervous or unsure we were of an answer and instead of helping us, they would ask another question that they knew we didn't know. Kids made fun of me, as I would faint in front of them. The teachers would tell my parents that I was a pretty good student but not one of the best in the class. In my mind, I saw myself as a shy stupid girl, who would never achieve anything. I felt no purpose here on the earth.

Third grade graduation. Age 9.
(Second row from bottom, second in line.)

GOD KNEW ME BEFORE I KNEW HIM

When I turned 14 years of age I had a choice to change schools. I could apply to attend a specialized high school that would educate me for college and prepare me for my future career. You can imagine what was going on in the mind of a 14 year old girl who always pictured herself on the back row, hiding behind everyone who was 'smart.' The first thing I said was, "I will make a fool of myself and everyone will laugh at me."

I was not a Christian at that time, but in the midst of it, God had a plan.

IF YOU HAVE GOD YOU HAVE EVERYTHING

Because I always loved drawing, painting and everything that had to do with art, I thought to apply to one of the art schools in the city. My parents' desire was for me to learn different languages. They felt it would be more useful than any pictures I could paint. As an obedient daughter I applied to both schools. During the summer break I was supposed to study art, Bulgarian and math in order to take the exams. While the summer days were rolling away, I was more concerned about studying art than math and Bulgarian. My enthusiasm to even apply at the language school was basically 'killed' when my

Part of the city of Veliko Turnovo.

former math teacher told my mom that I was not smart enough to learn any type of language and I would never be accepted because of my low grade in math. The Bulgarian school grades started at 2 (the lowest) and went up to 6 (the highest). My grade in Bulgarian was a 5 and in Math I had a 4.

Finally the time came when I had to take three tests in three weeks. The first one was in art. I was surprised when I was not accepted to attend the art school. There were only twenty-five openings. I was in a three-way tie for the last space. I was 28th on the list and no one wanted to give up their space. My only chance was to be accepted in the other school that had a reputation 'for smart kids only.' There was so much pressure on me that I thought I would fail before I even got started. I am amazed as I look back on those days when I didn't believe in God. I now believe that everything that took place was not an accident, but it had to be planned by Him. If you look back into your own life you will see that certain things happened and you really didn't have control over them. Some people call it luck, I call it purpose. As I said, God knows us before we are even born on this earth.

THE VICTORY

The day came for my Bulgarian exam. My mom came to encourage me that morning before I went in. The school was literally packed. There were over 1,000 kids and the spaces for each class were limited. I chose German as my first language and there were only 25 open spaces. I remembered that on the previous day a friend of mine gave me one of her notebooks. In it she explained the first chapter of one of the many books we were supposed to have read. Since I spent my whole summer painting pictures I didn't have time to read books. I only knew what I had read from that notebook the day before. As I walked into the classroom, on the black board were written two themes from two different books. My eyes caught a familiar title. It was the exact chapter from the book I had read in my friend's notes. The same thing happened with my math exam. When the test results were posted, I rushed to the school to see if I had been accepted. As you can already imagine, my name was on the list, under "German Language Class."

I came home and all my relatives and neighbors celebrated 'the victory' with me. There was such joy in my heart, that I was not a failure and that I would get the chance to speak another language. Up until that time we were required to study Russian, but for me that was never very hard since it's so similar to Bulgarian. This would be an opportunity for me to speak a language used in a Western European country.

NOW WHAT?

Are you wondering how this could relate to God predestining our lives? For me personally, He knew that I would not listen to anyone telling me about Jesus, and the opportunity to receive Him, unless it was someone from Germany or America. Studying German was the beginning of the preparation that led me to the Lord.

I was pretty young and didn't understand all the decisions I was about to face. My parents were just ordinary people who made enough money to take care of my grandparents and me. I remember the many late nights, when my mom would be sewing clothes to earn extra money. She was a schoolteacher with a special degree in sewing and fashion design. My father, on the other hand, was an engineer, who also had great abilities in building houses and repairing cars. All of my life, they sacrificially gave out of the little they had and instilled in me a determination to succeed. As their only child, I felt like I was capable of doing anything, but outside in the real world, I experienced feelings of insignificance and intimidation.

As I entered into my new classroom that fall, suddenly I was faced with the fear of, "Now that I am here, how am I going to prove that I am smart enough?" I could not have done it without my parent's encouragement and God coming to my rescue.
Later, my plan was to graduate and be a German translator for preachers and missionaries who came to Bulgaria. As you can see, coming to America was not a part of my plan. Yet, God's plan for me was not just to translate the revelations of another man, but to also have my own messages and to preach His Gospel. My life was about to make a complete turnaround.

GOD'S TASK IS ALWAYS BIGGER

"But the Lord said to me: "Don't say, 'I am a youth', for you shall go to all to whom I send you and whatever I command you, you shall speak. Don't be afraid of their faces, for I am with you,' says the Lord."" (Jer. 1:7)

We have all argued with God telling Him what we can and cannot do. One of the things I have learned from this passage and from the lives of many other men and women in the Bible, is that God always gave them a task bigger than themselves. When you have a vision bigger than your natural abilities, then it likely came from God and not from you. As long as you can do everything by relying only on your talents and abilities, you won't need God to help you because you have yourself. God gave Jeremiah a promise before he actually began to function as a prophet.

God gives you a promise so that you can hold on to it during the times when you don't see anything happening. The promises you receive from God will never involve only you, nor are they given to bring glory to you. They will always come to pass glorifying God in the end. During the fulfillment of a promise, He uses you to touch and change people's lives. A promise precedes the miracle, but the miracle witnesses of the promise. Let's continue remembering what God said:

> When you have a vision bigger than your natural abilities, then it likely came from God and not from you.

"Don't be afraid of their faces, for I am with you to deliver you." (Jer. 1:8)

IF YOU HAVE GOD YOU HAVE EVERYTHING

CHAPTER 2

IN SEARCH OF PURPOSE

There is a search for purpose in the heart of every human being on the earth. When we grow up without knowing our Creator - the One who made us and loved us before we even knew Him, we have an emptiness that no one or nothing else can fill. No matter how hard we might try to pretend that we don't think about life after death, or that we don't question the real meaning of our life, those questions are impossible to avoid in our mind at certain ages or certain circumstances. The truth is we all need something to believe in and someone to believe in us. The question is when you believe in something or someone, how do you know it's the only ultimate truth?

MY SCHOOLING

While growing up as a child I was always known to ask many questions, but no one seemed to know the answers. Many of us grew up believing that the Communist party was the only true 'god', and we had to obey its rules without hesitation. We had to be true to its ideas and dictation. I use the word dictation because we had to do what someone else told us to do without thinking or having a choice to express our ideas or opinions. If we did not willingly submit to their request there would be punishment.

Fear was a part of many people's lives. The thought that someone might betray you if they heard you talk bad about the Communist system kept you in constant turmoil. It was better not to ask questions and not to have ideas or public opinions. The goal of the Communist regime was to strip us from our rights as individuals and to leave us crippled without a vision or a dream for our lives. We didn't know why we were required to do what we did. We had to 'worship' the leaders and founders of the regime as well as their ideas even if they did not make sense to our minds. The word 'choice' was not in my vocabulary. There were no freedoms or liberties to take because every person in authority (teachers, bosses, policemen, etc.) decided what was best for the rest of us.

Having the opportunity to choose is a sign of freedom and equal rights, which did not exist during the time I was growing up in Bulgaria. Some people who opposed themselves against any of the Communist ideas were taken to concentration camps and were killed. Not many people knew that those camps existed until November 10, 1989, when the "Communist Giant" fell in Bulgaria.

What kind of system and what kind of 'god' would want to destroy a human life? It was not the God of Abraham, Isaac and Jacob. It was not the God who created us in His own image and gave us the power to choose. It was not the God who sent His Son, Jesus, to die for us that we might live with Him one day.[4] It was a 'god' made by a man, a false 'god' who appeared to be for us but was actually destroying us. Jeremiah 29:11 says,

"For I know the thoughts I think toward you, says the Lord, thoughts of peace and not evil, to give you a future and a hope."

That is the God I believe in.God's thoughts and plans for our lives are not burdensome but in our best interest. Today I know a God, whose name is Jesus and who gave all of us hope and a new future in Him.

Jesus' name was never mentioned in anything we did or celebrated. Christmas was not marked on the calendars as a Holiday, and Jesus was just another good man or a prophet who lived a long time ago.

PRAYERS THAT MAKE A DIFFERENCE

God had a plan for Bulgaria! Just as He has a plan for each one of us individually, He has a plan for each country. What was supposed to take place in order for the true God to show up on the scene? As I look back, I realize that the prayers of many caused the walls of Communism to come down. You may be one of them. I love what James 5:16b says,

"The effective, fervent prayer of a righteous man avails much."

The word effective could also be translated as "earnest, filled with energy prayer."[5] It's prayer that doesn't give up when things don't seem to be happening - a prayer that agrees with what God says and not a man's opinion. It was that kind of prayer that someone prayed over you and me before we came to know Jesus. When men or women who know their Savior start to really pray and intercede, the devil has no choice but to leave and release what he has taken into his possession.

Bulgaria was in the devil's possession for many years. You may ask why. The answer is simple. As long as we were under a Communist regime we could not hear about Jesus; the Gospel was not preached. Therefore the devil had total dominion over our lives. He is the one who is described in the Bible, as a thief who comes to steal, kill and destroy, but Jesus comes that we might have life, and have it more abundantly (John 10:10). By looking at the nation during those days the sign of a thief ruling was definitely there. People's rights were stolen, their hope was killed and their lives were destroyed. Bulgaria was in need of a Savior!

ABOUT MY COUNTRY

If you have studied geography you know that our country is pretty small, but beautiful. Bulgaria occupies 110,912 sq. km and at the present has a population of close to seven million people and is located in Eastern Europe: bordered by the countries of Rumania, Yugoslavia, Macedonia, Greece, Turkey and the Black Sea. Bulgaria is known for the awesome landscape of mountains rising up high with rivers and lakes surrounding them. Everywhere you turn, you are captivated by the natural beauty of the land.

Castle Tzarevetz
Veliko Turnovo, Bulgaria

Founded in 681 AD, Bulgaria was one of the first nations on the Eastern European Continent.[6] Two Slav brothers, Kiril and Metodii, introduced the alphabet to the Bulgarian people. The Bulgarian language uses the Slavic alphabet, which is also similar to the Russian alphabet.

The nation is known even to this day to have a very rich historical background with people who are willing to fight for their land. Because Bulgaria has fought many wars through the years, the battles they lost determined the shape of the territories we owned. For 500 years, Bulgaria was under the rulership of the Ottoman Empire.

Turkey, which represented the Ottoman Empire at that time, wanted Bulgaria to be a part of them by trying to force the Muslim religion on our nation. It was unsuccessful and in 865 A.D., the country was converted to Eastern Orthodox Christianity and translations of the Holy Scriptures were made from Greek into the Old-Bulgarian language, known as "Cyrillic Script."

A great historical moment took place during the Empire's reign. The Orthodox churches were used as a 'safe haven' when the Ottoman Empire came to kill people and destroy villages. One of the things I remember from my history classes is that the Bulgarian people would not betray their religion and national customs. Many who confessed to be Christians were killed during that era.

In 1877, prompted by the desire to expand toward the Mediteranian Sea and by Pan-Slavic sentiment, Russia declared war on the Ottoman Empire.[7] Russia defeated the Empire in 1878 and as a result of the victory the Bulgarian state was restored on March 3, 1878. Unfortunately, national integration was not attained. Western Macedonia and Thrace (the remainder of Macedonia) belonged to Bulgaria in the 13th century, but now remained under the rule of the Ottoman Empire. Bulgaria waged the Balkan war in 1912, joined by Serbia and Greece for the liberation of Thrace and Macedonia. We won that war against the Ottoman Empire, however we were defeated in the Second Balkan War. As a consequence, we lost considerable territory.[8]

On September 5, 1944 the Soviet Army invaded Bulgaria. No fighting occurred and the Bulgarian Government asked the USSR for a peace agreement (September 9, 1944). Under the protection of Soviet forces a government submissive to the USSR (Russia) was immediately established. This peace agreement provided for the control of Bulgaria and the evacuation of all Bulgarians from Yugoslav Macedonia and territories taken from Greece.[9] In 1946 we were proclaimed a republic. The Bulgarian Communist party came into power and the political parties were put under control. The economy and the banks were nationalized and the land was joined in co-operatives. Bulgaria remained among the USSR's most dependable allies.[10]

As you can see our country was never really free. The people were always suppressed and never found out what real freedom in the natural sense meant! Bulgaria was under Communism for the next 45 years. We had only one president for 30 years. His name was Todor Zhivkov. He would be the nominated candidate proposed during a special meeting of the ruling Communist party. Russia and Bulgaria continued to work together in building the new regime.

From the time I was born I can remember the gratitude everyone had for Russia for delivering us and helping us in everything we did. Most of the gas and machinery imports came from there. Russia was our 'big sister' that we all looked up to. We had only three TV channels, two in Bulgarian and one in Russian. We had very limited exposure to the outside world since each of the channels only broadcasted the news for three to four hours a day.

The Bulgarian channel "One", which was the one everyone watched, would start at 10:00 am and would end at 12:30 pm. In the evening it would begin at 5:30 pm and end at 12:30 am. The Russian channel "Three" would start at 8:00 pm and end at midnight. As you can see, there was not a lot of entertainment.

Most of the people understood the Russian language because we were required to study it from age seven until we graduated from High School. The news we heard on TV was mostly about our country and Russia. America was only mentioned briefly in certain debates and programs. In my mind it always sounded as though they and everyone else in the world hated us and were against us.

In order for us kids to have fun, we had to figure out our own games. We learned how to make the best out of what we had. Honestly, I was never bored. There was always something to do. We studied, played or hung around with our parents and grandparents. Our cultural intent was and still is to help one another. Families and relatives had close relationships and neighbors were best friends. But at the same time, no one fully trusted each other. Family business was usually not discussed out loud or in front of other people. The reason was 'the fear factor' as I said in the beginning of this chapter. When fear is the motivation behind every action and thought, we never feel free to be ourselves. The next three stories will show you that the Communist regime's goal was to strip us of our individuality and put everyone on the same level. The leaders were the head, and the people were just a crowd that had to follow.

ELEMENTARY SCHOOL

I was seven years old when I started kindergarten. My grandma usually walked me to the school, and my mom or dad picked me up. I took public transportation or walked everywhere I wanted to go.

One afternoon I ran home crying. A picture I had drawn in one of my art classes was placed all the way at the bottom of the blackboard as a sign of something I didn't do very well. As I said before, art was my favorite thing and for the teacher to tell me that I couldn't draw was devastating. At that time in my school you were not allowed to be left-handed and I was. No matter how hard I tried to draw with my right hand, my pictures looked awful. Many of the kids got slapped with the teacher's stick if they were found writing or drawing with their left hand. My mom talked to my teacher and I got special permission to draw with my left hand. Even with these special privileges for art, I had to learn to use my right hand for writing and everything else. I guess being left-handed was a sign of "sticking out of the crowd", so I was 'gently' pushed down!

When I entered into the first grade, we were required to wear uniforms, which showed that we belonged to the Communist party. It consisted of, a blue skirt for the girls and blue pants for the boys, white shirt, white socks, black shoes and a blue tie. After the third grade the blue tie was exchanged for a red one and we were required to wear it until we graduated

Age 6, with my grandparents, Milan and Irena Deminkovi, in my village, Koslovetz.

from High School. Everyday a teacher stood by the entrance of the school and checked to make sure we were wearing our blue or red tie. She checked to see if our nails were cut, if our hands were clean and if our shoes were polished. If nothing else, that taught me discipline and obedience to authority.

When grades were given we had to have our parents sign the report card. If we came to school and our parents had not signed our card, we were sent back home and asked to return with one of our parents. We were also sent home if we were not in proper uniform.

The biggest fear for me and my schoolmates was not the uniform check-in, but the classes we had. Some days we studied five different subjects and we went home with homework assignments in all of the classes. We had to know our lessons and do our homework everyday, because we might be asked to go up to the blackboard and say our lesson in front of all the other kids. Everyday was filled with fear for me that I might fail one of the subjects. As you already know I didn't just fail, I fainted in front of everyone. The teachers were to be feared and they were not to be our friends. If we were not obedient to them and they wrote a bad report in our file, it could influence our future career.

With grandma Mitka.
First day of school. Age 7.

LEARNING HOW TO CLEAN

One of the best stories I love to tell is how I learned to keep my room clean. You will probably laugh as you read about it. The teachers were required to come to our homes from time to time and inspect our rooms and desk. They had the freedom to open every single drawer in our rooms to check and see if it was in the right order. My clothes had to be folded, my books put on the right shelves, and my shoes in the proper place. One time I was in a hurry and I didn't take the time to clean my desk. I stuck everything that was on the top in the drawers hoping that my teacher would not check there. The first thing she did was to open the front drawer of my desk. Everything fell out. My assignment was to clean it up and to do extra homework for the next day.

I think everyone would have learned to be a "clean freak" under these circumstances. I call them "the dark ages." It appeared to be

43

a normal, simple life, but there was darkness in the nation that no one but Jesus could remove. Later, as I kept asking my parents and myself the question, "What is the purpose of our existence?" I soon came to the knowledge that they didn't know the answer. It was not something they were hiding from me; they were simply as lost in the darkness as I was.

DESPERATE FOR A HOPE AND A PURPOSE

I was so desperate for hope during my school years that I got involved in witchcraft. It was something that our whole class practiced. We thought we were calling the spirits of dead people to help us out in our studies and we didn't realize that we were messing around with real demons. Because I was afraid of what I saw take place in our little classroom meetings, I decided to walk away from it. I walked away from witchcraft, but the spirit of fear and depression followed me.

Right after I started studying at the Language School I became so depressed that I did not want to live any longer. From time to time we heard on the radio or saw on TV how some young person had committed suicide. I began to think these same thoughts. My life was going downhill, no one ever thought I would accomplish anything and there was no purpose driving me to live.

Our home in Veliko Turnovo.

We all have been there. You don't have to grow up under Communism to get discouraged or depressed. You don't even need to live under a certain regime to hate something or someone. You don't have to have a hard life like someone else to give up your hopes and your dreams. It's simply called being human. When life doesn't turn out the way we've imagined and dreamed, disappointment and hopelessness can creep in. The constant entertaining of negative thoughts will pull us into the downward spiral of despair.

God created us to be able to feel and express what is happening in our minds. When feelings are turned loose without any control over them they become dangerous. What then? If you live for God, you can ask Him to help you with what you are feeling and He will show you the right way to deal with those emotions. If you don't know Him, you allow the feelings to control your actions. I was desperate and the feelings of discouragement and hopelessness overtook my actions. It is in those weak moments the devil desires to snatch our lives away. It's also in those moments when God arrives on the scene. Was He too late for me?

> When life doesn't turn out the way we've imagined and dreamed, disap- pointment and hopelessness can creep in.

THE FALL OF THE COMMUNIST REGIME

Signs of freedom were in the air. The Berlin Wall that separated Eastern Germany from Western Germany fell on November 9, 1989. A day later, on November 10, 1989, it was announced on TV that the president of Bulgaria was forced to resign and the Communist regime was beginning to collapse. The news came as a shock to everyone. My city was located in the heart of Bulgaria. Situated in the foothills of Stara Planina (in English, "Old Mountain") Veliko Turnovo is one of the most visited places in the country, because of the history behind it. In school I studied about the struggles Bulgaria faced in trying to obtain freedom; now I was witnessing history being made before my eyes. People filled the streets in the center of the city, proudly waiving Bulgarian flags and singing national songs. Everyone was expressing the joy of freedom. My house was only a street away from all the activity the city was experiencing that night. From our garage terrace we could hear the shouting, singing, rumbling and clapping that was taking place in front of our National Theater. My family and neighbors ran down to join in the celebration. Soon the voices of individuals could no longer be distinguished, they sounded as though one person was saying, "Freedom, freedom, no more Communism."

I was almost 15 years old but I knew in my heart that Bulgaria had been awakened to a new future. It was exciting and yet scary because the familiar was no longer there. We had to learn to live in this new freedom, but there was no one to teach us what freedom really meant.

Veliko Turnovo, Bulgaria

In the following months many of the statues and museums that were built by the Communist leaders were destroyed. Red represented the color of dictatorship but blue was the color of democracy. Many blue flags flew everywhere, yet the Bulgarian people were still under oppression. What was known as freedom was taking the shape of chaos.

THE FIRST TIME I SAW A BIBLE

Weeks passed by. The future was before us, but we didn't know what to do with it. One afternoon I was walking back from school, when I saw a lady selling Bibles on the street. That was the first time I had seen a Bible out in public. The Orthodox Church was also awakened at that time. Many of the priests started to talk more about God. We remained a nation classified as Christian even under Communism, but there was just one little problem - most of the people didn't even believe in God. It wasn't a matter of the heart, but rather a religious status. If you were born in Bulgaria you were automatically an Orthodox Christian and if you were born in Turkey you would be a Muslim. No one ever mentioned that you needed to have a relationship with Jesus by accepting Him in your heart and making Him your personal Lord and Savior. Because of the way the priests talked about the Lord I was actually afraid of 'their god.' In my mind I pictured Him as a mean being that wanted to make me sad.

> We had to learn to live in this new freedom, but there was no one to teach us what freedom really meant.

While I was standing on the street staring at the Bible, an older man walked by, looked in my eyes and said: "There is a God whose name is Jesus and He loves you." I didn't believe him. As a matter of fact I replied that I didn't care. A few days after that incident took place, I was at the end of my rope and I wanted to take my life. I walked back and forth in my room as I made my plans. I grabbed for the knife and in that instant the words of the older man began to run through my mind. "What if there was a God, like he said and what if He did love me? What then? I have to find out." I couldn't wait any longer. Jesus had to find me right now!

THE POWER OF GOD'S WORD

As I write I am reminded of Isaiah 55:11,

> *"So shall My Word be that goes forth from My mouth; It shall not return to Me void. But it shall accomplish what I please, and it shall prosper in the thing for which I sent it."*

In Hebrews 4:12, the Word of God is described as "living and powerful, and sharper than any two-edged sword, piercing even to the division of soul and spirit, and of joints and marrow, and is a discerner of the thoughts and intents of the heart." What took place in my heart at that moment was God's word was at work.

When you speak God's word, it has power to divide between the truth and the lie. It's so powerful that it can take you out of the snare of the enemy and bring you into the full knowledge of God. There were no coincidences in my life. The Word of God with the truth that Jesus actually loved me kept me until the day I heard the whole Gospel. My grandmother's sister Verka, has believed in Jesus since she was a young girl. Many times she came over to the

> God's Word always brings forth fruit. You can't lose when you know God and when you declare His Word over situations and over relationships!

house and told us about the Lord. I never paid attention to her, but her prayers and words were the first seeds that were planted in my heart. The words of the man on the street only reminded me of what my aunt had told me. God knew 'my number' and He was going to rescue me.

The Word of God is like a seed that gets planted in our hearts and starts to work its way up. When you pray for friends and relatives who appear to not listen when you talk to them about Jesus, do not worry. As long as you speak God's Word to them in a way they can understand, the Holy Spirit will continue to use it and bring it up in their thoughts and cause them to turn and cry out to Him. God's Word always brings forth fruit. You can't lose when you know God and when you declare His Word over situations and over relationships!

It's powerful to know how much God cares for us as individuals and that He has the power over regimes, graven images by people and over the darkness that is over nations. He was not going to leave out Bulgaria; He was not going to forget about us. His plan was for good and not for evil. We were close to finding out what real hope and freedom meant.

IF YOU HAVE GOD YOU HAVE EVERYTHING

CHAPTER 3

TIME TO CHOOSE

I could feel the pain pierce through my shoulders and move down my lower back. I had been carrying my backpack full of my schoolbooks for my daily subjects for almost three hours and it was starting to show its effect on me. The stores and the streets seemed really crowded with people that day. I could hear music down the corner but I couldn't make my way there because of all the people walking around. As I walked down the street, I saw a friend in the crowd and I stopped to talk about what might be taking place. Some young people came and handed us little brochures. When I looked at the teens' faces they looked like they were from another country. On the back of all three brochures I read the following, "Produced by Latter Day Saints", "Produced by the Jehovah's Witnesses", "Produced by Hare Krishna Followers."

All of the brochures had something in common and that was the name of Jesus. He was mentioned in all three of them, yet something did not seem right to me. A little bit confused, we continued to walk down the street, but this time we decided to take the crosswalk on the other side of the road because there were fewer people walking there. We had just crossed over when two girls stopped by and handed us another brochure. On this one we read that we were invited to a service with drama, music and special guests from Germany and America. The meeting was held close by so we decided to investigate.

MEETING A GROUP FROM GERMANY

Just a few days prior, we had a group from Germany on our street distributing food. I was in my first year of studying German and I wanted to practice my German skills. I went out to talk to the teens and leaders of the group. They gave us a huge box full of food they had brought over from Western Germany.

Market place - "Pazar"
Veliko Turnovo, Bulgaria

Bulgaria was going through a major economic crisis. Starting at the beginning of 1990 and through 1992 there was very limited amounts of food in the stores. The prices were skyrocketing and people were losing their jobs. The changes and the surviving lifestyle continued even after 1992. Food shortage was all over the country and we had to have coupons to buy our groceries. Monthly, every family got one food coupon per person. Each coupon was good for sugar, oil, flour, bread and rice. For example, when a shipment of rice came to town, many people would rush to stand in line to redeem their rice coupons. A box of food for us as a family meant not having to wait in lines for the next few weeks.

I found out that the German people were Christians who had been praying for Bulgaria. When they heard of the opportunity to come and visit our nation they decided to bring in food and clothing. My family and I were speechless as we were looking through the box finding all these awesome foods that we were never able to afford. In the bottom of the box I saw at least ten different chocolates. I love chocolate. My mom would buy a bar for me when she had some extra money. I would eat it in small portions for weeks at a time. Now that I had ten bars I was overjoyed. Right beside the chocolates was a Bible almost like the one I saw being sold on the street. I took it into my hands and was so excited to hold it for the first time in my life. I was almost 16 years old. The teens told me that they would be in the city doing drama and singing for the next few days, but they didn't say where. They just said, "We'll see each other again." Since I wanted to practice my German, I was determined to find them.

> I love chocolate. My mom would buy a bar for me when she had some extra money. I would eat it in small portions for weeks at a time.

WE ARE IN THE RIGHT PLACE

The brochure the teens handed us caused me to think that this group might be the same people that gave us the box of food. I was eager to get to the theater. Finally we walked in. It was totally packed. Over 500 people were sitting down and many others were just standing around. By some miracle we found two empty seats five minutes before the performance began. While people were getting up on the stage I saw some familiar faces. I was excited as I recognized them as the same German group I saw just a few days earlier. We were in the right place!

THE MIRACLE THAT LEAD ME
TO BELIEVE IN GOD

The music and the drama began. One thing was evident throughout that evening – God was real. We were taught that He loved us and gave His Son (Jesus) for us, so that we might be forgiven and freed from our sins. Jesus wanted to be our friend. We needed to accept Him in our heart and confess Him with our mouth as a personal Lord and Savior. The man preaching that night was from America, but was speaking in German. His name was Paul Stern.

Now, can you see God's plan at work when I was accepted to study in the Language school? Paul Stern and his wife Eleanor came over together with the other German group and they wanted to help us and tell us the good news. Everything he said was so simple, but powerful. I could understand it before it was translated. All the thoughts and questions I had in my mind about life after death and our purpose here on the earth were answered. Still, there was something in me that didn't want to fully trust all he was saying. I wanted to see if God knew me personally. I had a persistent stomach pain and I wanted to see if God would heal me. That would prove to me that He is real. As I was thinking that, Pastor Paul said, "God loves you so much, He wants to heal you tonight. He wants to heal your heart and your body." In that same instant the pain in my stomach left. I remember it so clearly to this day. It was a turning point in my life. I knew God was alive! He was not just someone who lived a long time ago. He was not a picture on the wall at a church. He was a God who knew me personally.

The opportunity was given for people to receive Him in their heart as their Lord and Savior. I was one of the first ones to run down the aisle. Many people followed. Soon there were more of us standing down where the pulpit was and only a few were left in their seats. The people from Germany and America came to each one of us. Tears were streaming down their cheeks. They hugged us and prayed with us. We were like sheep with no shepherd. We were scattered everywhere, afraid of everyone and everything but in one instant the truth was made known to us. We just had our first choice, to accept Him or to reject Him.

NEW RESTRICTIONS

It seemed like many people became Christians in those days. The first two and a half years after the Communist regime lost its power, missionaries from Western Europe and America came to preach the Gospel to us and distribute food. Later, new restrictions were imposed, but they continued to come. With so many missionaries coming to Bulgaria, many occult groups were also seeking to find new members. Things were taking place so fast that the government didn't know what to do. In their desire for protection over the nation they made an announcement that every teaching outside of the Orthodox Church would be considered occult. Evangelical Churches were labeled as occults and were considered to be equal to the teachings of the Jehovah Witnesses, Mormons, Hare Krishna, and every other teaching that was using Jesus in their vocabulary.

THE MESSAGE OF THE CROSS

A great deception began to rule everywhere. If you were not an Orthodox Christian, you were considered to have accepted the teachings of a different culture and with that you had betrayed the Bulgarian traditions and beliefs. Because of what we heard on the radio, TV and read in the newspapers, my parents soon began to question if I was involved in one of the occult organizations. My Aunt Verka, her daughter's family, and I were the only ones who believed in God in my entire family. The rest of our relatives, including my parents and grandparents, didn't want to hear the name of Jesus mentioned in any conversation. In school I was the only one in my class who believed in God and attended an Evangelical Church. The news that I had lost my mind and was an Evangelical Christian soon spread among my schoolmates.

It was during this time that I learned how to know God and what He could do. Nothing would convince my parents, relatives and friends to believe in God unless they saw a drastic change in my life. I was still very much a Bulgarian. The only difference was that I loved the Lord. I decided to be an example to them. I prayed that one day they too would come to know Him the same way I knew him. It was not a religion that was going to save them, but the power of God.

> *"For the message of the cross is foolishness to those who are perishing, but to us who are being saved it is the power of God. For it is written: I will destroy the wisdom of the wise, and bring to nothing the understanding of the prudent. Where is the wise? Where is the scribe? Where is the disputer of this age? Has not God made foolish the wisdom of this world? Because the foolishness of God is wiser than men, and the weakness of God is stronger than men. But God has chosen the foolish things of the world to put to shame the wise, and God has chosen the weak things of the world to put to shame the things which are mighty."*
> *(1Cor. 1:18-20,25,27)*

What seems wise in our eyes as humans is foolishness to God. He takes you and me, the ones who have been rejected by society's standards and declares that He will use us to put to shame all those who think of themselves as wise.[11] So many times we read something in the Bible, and we don't believe it or don't take it as though it's the truth. The Bible is not just a book for us receive comfort when we are down, but it has power, and it is not just some spooky unknown power, but it comes straight from God.

FAITH COMES FROM GOD'S WORD

It really doesn't matter how much of the Bible you can quote, but how much of what you know you believe and practice daily in your life.

"Faith comes by hearing and hearing by the Word of God." *(Rom. 10:17)*

It really doesn't matter how much of the Bible you can quote, but how much of what you know you believe and practice daily in your life.

When you hear God's Word faith begins to grow inside of you. You can have faith in many different things. For instance people believe and could put their trust in the stock market. By daily watching their investments grow, their faith begins to grow that one-day they will become wealthy. In a split second the stock market drops and their faith begins to waver. You cannot feed your faith based on natural things and what makes sense to your mind. Faith is supernatural.[12]

"Faith is the substance of things hoped for, the evidence of things not seen." (Heb. 11:1)

We all need faith that sees beyond the natural into the supernatural where God is. Faith is not to be put into men, a government or a nation. Faith is to be put in God through Jesus Christ and His Word. When our faith is plugged into God's Word, only then can that Word begin to work in us and for us.

I have met many people who have a Bible in their homes, but they have never read it. I have also talked to others who read the Bible because that is what their church or religion teaches them to do. I have come to the conclusion, that if we do certain things for God without the desire being there, then that becomes a tradition and religion. We are to obey God and read the Word, not because we are told to by men, but simply because we love Him. That along with the daily miracles He does is what makes Christianity different from other religions. We can choose to love and serve God. Others are forced to believe in their 'god.'

Jesus is not just some religion, nor is He a religious church organization. He knows you with all the good and the bad that is in you. He is the only One, who will never betray you, who will always stand beside you and who will always believe the best in you. That is what I came to understand in the days when no one believed anything I said about Him. Soon my family and friends discovered something they didn't know.

> Jesus is not just some religion, nor is He a religious church organization. He knows you with all the good and the bad that is in you.

MANY CHANGES

The days were rolling by. I went to school but there was something different in me. I had such joy in my heart. The more I read the Bible the more I realized that I really was on God's winning team. I asked

God to give me His wisdom for the subjects that were difficult for me and He did. All my grades started to improve and soon the teachers noticed the difference. I was relaxed when I got up to speak and studying German became much easier.

In all my classes I had the chance to witness about God's power working in my life. In most of the essays I wrote for my German and Bulgarian classes, I talked about God and His plan for our lives. In my home I put scriptures everywhere so that when guests and relatives came to visit they had an opportunity to read them and ask questions. I was not ashamed or afraid to share my faith with them. God did so much for me. The thoughts of depression were gone. Now I had purpose in my life. No one could convince me that God did not exist because I had a first hand opportunity to experience His power. In spite of it all I still didn't know what was going to take place and what God's big plan was, but I had to take it one day at a time.

GOD'S VOICE

I continued attending the Evangelical Church in my town, Veliko Turnovo, and grew in the Lord. There were so many things about prayer and hearing God's voice that I didn't know. My greatest desire at that time was to know God better. If He was my best friend, I had to learn how to talk to Him. I struggled in my prayer time. I couldn't think of what to really say to God. My longest prayer was five minutes. If you are wondering why I am taking you into depth, my answer to you is simple. I learned that hearing from God and recognizing His voice is a process. Also, learning to pray is a process. You grow in it and

> Also, learning to pray is a process. You grow in it and the more you do it the better you get at it.

the more you do it the better you get at it. Some people could look at particular leaders' lives today and assume that they all had great abilities and confidence from the time they were kids. Not necessarily. The ability to hear God's voice will come as you study the Bible and renew your mind. Renewing for me meant exchanging. Exchanging the old patterns of thinking for the things God said about me. It was a process and took time, as you will see as you read through the rest of the chapters. No matter what level you are on concerning your relationship with God and your ability to hear His voice, there will always be room for improvement, especially when you go through problems and obstacles. Those are the times that draw us closer to Him!

FILLED

One night I was staying up late, looking at different scriptures, trying to hear God's voice. The particular passage I read was in Acts 2:1-4,

> *"When the Day of Pentecost had fully come, they were all with one accord in one place. And suddenly there came a sound from heaven, as of a rushing mighty wind, and it filled the whole house where they were sitting. Then there appeared to them divided tongues, as of fire, and one sat upon each of them. And they were all filled with the Holy Spirit and began to speak with other tongues, as the Spirit gave them utterance."*

As a 'baby' Christian, most of what I read didn't make much sense, but in my heart I knew I wanted to have what those disciples had. The pastor at church mentioned that in two days we would celebrate the day of Pentecost and they were going to pray for people to be filled with the Holy Spirit. I couldn't wait two days! As I was going to bed, I simply told God that I don't understand everything but would like to speak in other languages. If He wanted to do that, then I would like to wake up in the morning with that gift.

And so the morning came. I woke up and while I was still in bed, I said, "God, I am ready when you are." It's kind of funny to think of the way I talked to God at that time, but as I said, I didn't want to pretend to be someone I was not. I opened my mouth and all of a sudden it was like a river coming out of me. Words that weren't making sense to my mind were coming out of my mouth. It was something I couldn't explain, but it was reality. I knew God had baptized me in His Holy Spirit.

From that day my countenance began to change and my prayer language took a leap. When I didn't exactly know what to say to God and how to say it, I would begin to use my prayer language. My prayers no longer seemed to go up, bounce off the ceiling and come down. I still spoke my heart and mind, but the Holy Spirit was showing me scriptures I could use in my prayers. Jesus always referred to the Holy Spirit as the Helper, the Teacher, and the Spirit of truth.

> "But when the Helper comes, whom I shall send to you from the Father, the Spirit of truth who proceeds from the Father, He will testify of Me. And you also will bear witness, because you have been with Me from the beginning."
> (John 15:26-27)

That's why the Holy Spirit was sent to us, so that in the times when we need help, He is beside us. The word "Helper" comes from 'parakletos' and it means, "Called to one's side." It signifies an intercessor, comforter, helper, advocate and counselor.[13] The Holy Spirit is the one who gives us strength to endure until we see a promise fulfilled. He is also the one who reveals to us what the Word of God means. He gives us revelation knowledge, or simpler said, He opens up our spiritual eyes to understand God's Word. I discovered that praying in the Spirit meant "speaking mysteries to God." My natural words couldn't express what I needed to say, therefore, the new prayer language helped me to communicate with God my feelings, concerns and desires that were deep down in my heart. (1Cor. 14:2-4)

The more I prayed in the Holy Spirit the stronger I became on the inside and I had greater confidence that God was not only going to hear my prayers, but He would answer them, when they were in accordance to His will for my life.

> *"Now this is the confidence that we have in Him, that if we ask anything according to His will, He hears us. And if we know that He hears us, whatever we ask, we know that we have the petitions that we've asked of Him."*
> *(1John 5:14-15)*

It's easy to say that God answered almost every prayer I prayed at that time, but that was not actually true. God seemed to "pamper" me with many blessings early in my walk with Him. Changes in my life brought me great joy as well as heartache. God remained with me through everything.

> *"For whatever is born of God overcomes the world. And this is the victory that has overcome the world-OUR FAITH."*
> *(1 John 5:4)*

The faith we place in our God will always cause us to be victorious, even in the times of the impossible.

CHAPTER 4

ACCEPTING GOD'S CALL

The year of 1992 was filled with many personal experiences and testimonies of God's power working in my life. I read about Peter in Matthew 14:22-33, who after hearing Jesus call him out of the boat, stepped on the water and started walking over the waves of the sea. Every time I read something from the Bible I took it as though it could happen to me today. I could feel that the time was coming for *me* to learn how to walk on the water and not just sit in the boat of familiarity. The sea for me didn't exist as natural water, but of insecurities, rejection from people and most of all fear of the unknown. I was comfortable in my type of "boat", which included translating for German groups and ministers who would come to our nation to preach the Gospel. Up to that time I had some public exposure, but by no means did I feel prepared for the plan of God for my life that I was about to discover.

A CALL TO PREACH THE GOSPEL

The year slowly rolling by, and we entered into the new 1993. I was 17 years of age and had only one year left to graduate High School. Just like everyone else in my class I was beginning to make plans for the future. Would I go to Germany and study there or should I apply at the university in my city? It was normal to think that the next door God would open for me would be connected with the German language.

It was one of those days, which I am sure you have also had from time to time, when you just stare out of the window and dream away. That was actually one of my favorite things to do when I was a kid. My desk faced the window that overlooked the hills and the mountains of the city. Every time I took a break from studying I went to the balcony connected to my room and look at the houses, the people walking outside, and the old castle far away on the hill, where the Bulgarian kings used to live. At one time my city had been the capital of Bulgaria and the castle later on was transformed into a historical attraction. At night there would be a light show mixed with music in the background and a short history of Bulgaria.

> I could feel that the time was coming for me to learn how to walk on the water and not just sit in the boat of familiarity.

The day that God came and interrupted my 'dreaming session' was actually a cold winter's day. You couldn't see anything else outside except the big snowflakes coming down and covering the dark ground. I had read in Mark 16:15-18 where Jesus gave the disciples the great commission to go out and preach His Gospel.

"He said to them, 'Go into all the world and preach the Gospel to every creature. He who believes and is baptized will be saved, but he who does not believe will be condemned. And these signs will follow those who believe: In My name they will cast out demons, they will speak with new tongues; they will take up serpents; and if they drink anything deadly, it will by no means hurt them; they will lay hands on the sick, and they will recover."

There are times when you can read a certain verse or chapter in the Bible and suddenly 'the lights come on' in your mind. No matter how many times I had read that passage, up until that night I had never pictured myself traveling or preaching in front of people. I was only a translator. In verse 20 of the same chapter it said, "And they went out and preached everywhere, the Lord working with them and confirming the word through the accompanying signs. Amen." Immediately something inside me jumped and I said, "God, I don't want to do anything else in my life, but travel and preach the Gospel like the disciples. I want to be used by You!" I almost shocked myself as I said it out loud. I guess, you could say, my 'boat days' were over and I was getting ready to step out where Jesus was calling my name. I knew deep down in my heart that it was a part of His plan for my life.

It happened so fast and in an instant. No one laid hands on me, no one prophesied and I didn't hear an audible voice from heaven. God simply placed a desire in my heart to do it while reading His Word. For the first time I saw myself standing before many people telling them about Jesus. I was excited but also scared. What if I failed in trying to walk on the water of uncertainties? How would I get from point "A" to point "Z?" Too many changes had to take place.

"HOW COULD I DO THIS?"

At that time I didn't know of many women preachers and the questions that started to rush through my mind were too overwhelming for me to answer. I wrote everything down in my journal and kept it to myself. My parents wouldn't understand what I was talking about even if I told them and my friends at school would probably laugh at me. As I continued to read in the book of Acts about the disciples going out to cities and nations preaching and healing people my faith took another leap. I realized that being only a good example for my parents and relatives was not going to be enough. I had to have more testimonies of God's miraculous power in my life. I didn't know what I was praying for.

> Jesus never promised that we would have a "problem-free, instant-miracle life-style" after we got saved or after we decided to obey Him.

Before there is a testimony, we always face a problem. Jesus never promised that we would have a "problem-free, instant-miracle lifestyle" after we got saved or after we decided to obey Him. What He did say was:

"Come to Me, all you who labor and are heavy laden, and I will give you rest. Take My yoke upon you and learn from Me, for I am gentle and lowly in heart, and you will find rest for your souls. For my yoke is easy and My burden is light."
(Matt. 11:28-30)

The rest we find in God can only be experienced when we relax and allow Him to carry us while we are in the midst of the problems. As long as I did those things He said to me, then I accepted the yoke, which was the requirement He had for me and not someone else. Therefore no matter how heavy the burden seemed He was the one who was carrying it for me. The next few months were filled with a few 'waves' and opportunities for God to calm the storms in my life.

WHY DID I SAY "YES"?

My small hesitation to fully run after God's call on my life came to an end a month later. It was February 1993. After a second stroke, my dad's father was paralyzed in his left arm and leg. His health wasn't improving and we all knew that his time to leave us was fast approaching. He was my favorite grandpa and I loved him very much. My mom's father had passed away when I was still a young child. Most of the memories I have are from the days when I played with my grandpa Milan. I knew I had to go and see him and tell him about Jesus.

When I walked in his room, he was so sick that he didn't remember me right away. Finally, when he came back to full consciousness, I started telling him about life after death and how much Jesus loved him. He asked some questions like, "Why if there is God, I am sick? Why can't I see God like I see you?" I knew I couldn't give him a full explanation, not because I didn't want to, I just didn't know how. The only thing I could say was, "I don't know the answers to those questions, but what I know is that He really does love you. He is real and wants you to be with Him in heaven." As I said that, I looked at my grandpa. He had closed his eyes and was no longer aware of what I was saying. There are no words to explain how broken my heart was. With overwhelming emotions of sadness and helplessness, I left his room.

Here I was, wanting to preach the Gospel, but didn't know how to answer those simple, but hard for me questions. I didn't know how to even lead a person in the prayer of salvation. My grandpa died a week later. I was devastated. I had prayed that somehow after I had left his room his spiritual eyes would be opened to see the truth.

Now, he was gone, and I wasn't sure if he ever asked Jesus into his heart.

The reality of heaven and hell hit me. Both places were so real and there was no way you can change things after death. According to the teachings of the Orthodox Church, even if someone died, you could still help them get to heaven by praying to one of the saints and lighting candles. I guess that could make you feel better, but I knew it was not what the Bible said. In Galatians 3:16 I read,

> *"knowing that a man is not justified by the works of the law but by faith in Jesus Christ, even we have believed in Christ Jesus, that we might be justified by faith in Christ and not by the works of the law; for by the works of the law no flesh shall be justified."*

Jesus was the only one who fulfilled the law and only through faith in Him we are forgiven from our sins and have eternal life with Him.

The day my grandpa passed away was the day I decided that no matter who I was and what I could or couldn't do I would not allow another one of my relatives or friends to die without me being able to share the Gospel with them. I knew I couldn't save them, only God could, but I needed to know how to share Jesus in a way they would respond. If I was going to preach God's word in front of people I had to do something more than just read, pray and be excited about it. I had to act on what I felt in my heart was to be my destiny.
God used that particular incident in my life to open my eyes so that I could see the world and the people around me in a different light.

> *"And when Jesus went out He saw a great multitude; and He was moved with compassion for them, and healed their sick."* (Matt. 14:14)

If Jesus was my greatest friend and teacher, I had to do what He did, in spite of the way I felt and thought about myself. He didn't just see the multitudes of people, He went out and healed them, He fed them, He taught them and He loved them. I was finding out that compassion was exactly what brought those missionaries over to our nation. Because they allowed that compassion to control them I heard the Gospel. It was not just a feeling of deep emotion or pity, but it was love expressed through actions. I had to take my focus off of me and look at people through God's eyes in order for His healing power to fully flow through my life.

GOD'S PLAN IS UNFOLDING

Since I was already half way out of my 'boat', after graduating from the Language School in the summer of 1994, I made the decision that I would go to a Bible School rather than study at a university. My parents were very disappointed and worried that I was about to make some wrong decisions. I had applied at two Bible Schools in Germany but I wasn't accepted at either one. I wasn't sure what to do next. God had to reveal to me the next chapter of the plan. Looking back now, I can see how my steps were ordered by the Lord.

He had brought two missionary couples from the States to work with the Evangelical Church in our city. Bonnie and Randy Downing from Danville, IL, came to my country in 1992 and served as my youth pastors. Mike and Ruth Matthews from Altoona, KS, were in our city for over a year and were traveling and ministering at different churches across Bulgaria. It was during that summer of decisions that Mike and Ruth talked to me and a friend of mine about Victory Bible Institute (VBI) in Tulsa, OK. It sounded like a great Bible school that was located not far from where they lived in the United States. Their plans were to go back to the USA that fall and study at the Missions school that was a part of VBI. Since I didn't speak English I wasn't even thinking about going to the USA to study, so I simply

IF YOU HAVE GOD YOU HAVE EVERYTHING

disregarded that option. God did not, though, and my life was going to be rocked by what I discovered to be His will for me.

That same day while thinking that it might be nice to go over for a visit, God said to me, "You are not going only for a visit; Victory Bible Institute is the place I have for you and where you will be studying." I will not exaggerate if I say that after that statement I was speechless and astonished. The answer from God came to me as a thought, but this was not my usual way of thinking. It was clear, strong and affirming. My heart was beating fast and I knew God was the one speaking to me. Still, it didn't make sense to me. I wanted to do great things for God but when He actually answered my request, I got scared. "God, why would I go to a nation so far away when I can't even speak their language?"

MY THOUGHTS BROUGHT WORRY, HIS VOICE BROUGHT PEACE

That night I gave God five reasons why I couldn't do it. The first one was that I didn't speak English and I wouldn't be able to understand anything. Not only that, but I had no money, nor did my parents. It was very hard to get a visa for the United States and my parents, since they weren't Christians, probably would not allow me to go anyway.

My mind was soon quieted down with God's answers. "I know all languages and can give you a supernatural ability to speak and understand English. I also have all the money in the world that you will ever need. I am bigger than any government and officials and I am the One who will give you a visa to go to America. When you obey me, your parents will come to know Me, your relatives will begin to get saved and I will open all the doors for you to preach the Gospel in other nations."

That night God gave me a promise much greater than all the excuses I had. If you had an offer like that, it would be hard to resist. I finally said that I would go. In spite of the fact that I wasn't totally sure how all those details would work out, that night God placed supernatural faith in me to believe that what He said to me was going to take place and I didn't have to worry or figure it out. How could I figure out God's plan? It was bigger than what I could ever dream or imagine!

The next morning I woke up still in shock and I rushed over to Mike and Ruth's home to tell them what God had said. One of my friends translated for us. God had already prepared their hearts to help me get to the United States and study at the Bible College, so the news I had was not a big shock to them.

The summer flew by. I was planning to arrive in the United States in December of 1994. I had only three short months to apply at VBI (Victory Bible Institute), get their acceptance letter, learn the language, get a visa, buy a ticket and fly over. Even though it looked impossible in my eyes, I knew that it was possible for God.

HOW DO YOU KNOW WHEN GOD SPEAKS?

I have always believed that when God calls you to do something bigger than your natural abilities, He will give you the faith to believe it; you will have supernatural peace in your heart and confidence that He is able to do it.[14] That doesn't mean that you will never doubt or get discouraged. You probably will, just like everyone else in the Bible. You are not perfect and you are also still very much a human being. It's in those times when your mind doesn't make sense to you that there will be an assurance in your heart that God is working on your behalf.

Many times people take risks or make decisions based on someone else's experiences with the Lord. When we don't have a 'Rhema' word from God, or in other words a 'spoken word' by Him, a personal revelation of His promise, then it is very possible for us to make fools of ourselves, by pursuing our own agenda or desiring to copy someone else. What do I mean by saying a "Rhema" word? I think it's important for me to take time and explain it, so you will be able to clearly understand where I'm coming from and what happened in my life.

'Rhema' actually originates from the Greek and was used by Jesus in Matthew 4:4, when He encountered Satan's temptations in the wilderness,[15]

> "But He answered and said, 'It is written, Man shall not live by bread alone, but by every word that proceeds from the mouth of God.'"

In this verse in the original Greek 'Rhema' is used to describe the personal communicated word to us. The Bible as a whole represents the 'Logos' word, which is the message God gave to all of us. 'Rhema' is the communication of that message and usually includes a scripture, perhaps passages of God's Word that will be illuminated in our mind and spirit while reading the 'Logos' word. Sometimes, as you already read, I had 'Rhema' words, while studying His word and other times, God spoke to me without using a scripture. In the second case, the word I heard had to be in agreement with what His written word said. 'Rhema' is personal and only applies to you.

In Ephesians 6:10-18, Paul was encouraging us to put on the whole armor of God. Part of that armor included the helmet of salvation in vs. 17 and the sword of the Spirit, which was the Word of God. The meaning of the 'word' of God is not the actual 'Logos' word, but was the personal 'Rhema' word, the same one Jesus used to rebuke Satan in Matt. 4:4. Therefore, when we speak or confess something from God's 'Logos' Word, which has not become a 'Rhema' word for us, it will have no power and meaning behind it. It will not produce results. God will not do anything He didn't promise us, but when a promise is given only then He is obligated to perform it.

How do you know if you have a promise from God? It will always line up with the 'Logos' word in the Bible, and will glorify God at the end. It will also bring an encouragement to you and cause you to walk by faith and not by sight. Our faith becomes alive when God speaks a personal 'Rhema' word to us.[16] When you know that you have received a promise, a true 'Rhema' word from Him, you don't need to go around and ask people if they agree with it, because they probably won't. It's not their promise it's yours!

> How do you know if you have a promise from God? It will always line up with the 'Logos' word in the Bible, and will glorify God at the end. It will also bring an encouragement to you and cause you to walk by faith and not by sight.

I've learned over the years, starting from the time I lived in Bulgaria, that when God speaks something to me, He usually won't inform everyone else about my business. If I were to share a personal promise in order to receive people's approval soon or later I will frustrate myself and very possibly talk myself out of it. Because our natural mind is used to doing the things that are logical, I had to write down what God spoke to me so I wouldn't forget it and so that reasoning or doubt would not snatch God's promise from my heart.

THE FIRST STEPS 'ON THE WATER'

The time came for me to take my first steps on the water. I found a great comfort as I read Gen. 12 and the way God spoke to Abraham. He was called to leave his country and the Lord promised to make him a father of many nations. Sarah and Abraham were scared, I am sure, and they weren't perfect either. Genesis 16, talks about the conception of Ishmael, who was Abraham's son conceived by his Egyptian maidservant, Hagar. Ishmael will always stand for something we produce on our own, out of fear perhaps, or sometimes because of a lack of patience. Isaac on the other hand stands for the supernatural. He was the promised son and was born out of faith and trust in God.

I had questions: "How do I wait on God? Is waiting equal to sitting around and doing nothing?" Since I knew how to study languages, I decided to take the first step and learn how to read in English. God's part was to give me an understanding. I would read different words from the dictionary and I would automatically remember their meaning and pronunciation without having to write them down. It took me five years to learn German and I learned how to read in English in less than a month. My mind couldn't explain it, but it was reality.

The approval letter from Victory Bible Institute came at the end of October and my next step was to go to the Embassy for my student visa for the United States. God continued to give me an understanding of what I read in English and my faith took another leap. When I made the announcement that I was going to the States to study, my parents and all my other relatives were in shock. No one from my family had lived anywhere outside of Bulgaria, and for me to travel to the States appeared foolish and impossible. On top of that, I didn't look like one of those "independent kids" that knew everything about life. Their response actually encouraged me to pray more and I was more determined to do what God had asked of me to do. Now that I had publicly announced that I was going, I couldn't stop half way.

> "And we know that all things work together for good for those who love God, to those who are the called according to His purpose." (Rom. 8:28)

That was one of the many verses I read to myself during those three months in order to keep my faith alive and to encourage myself when thoughts of doubt would try to come to my mind. Just because I had a promise from God, didn't mean that I was automatically immune to the attacks of the enemy. The waves in the sea of life appeared pretty big, but my focus had to be on Him who called me out.

IF YOU HAVE GOD YOU HAVE EVERYTHING

CHAPTER 5

CAN HE PART A "RED SEA" FOR ME?

November 1994. It was a cold morning and my hands and toes were slowly getting numb from the freezing wind. My friend and I had been waiting in front of the American Consulate in Sofia for close to three hours. The day for me to get my visa for the States had arrived. Over 100 other people were in line that day and I could feel my heart pounding and fear began to show its grips on my voice. You could hear people talking while stomping with their feet to keep warm.

Our country was going through a major economic crisis and many people were trying to find jobs abroad in order to make money and take care of their families. To get a visa for the United States seemed like one of the most impossible things for me. Every person in that line had a desire to go to America. Who would they allow to go and who would they stop? I could feel some of the same emotions rising in me from the days when I was in high school and I would be asked to go up to the blackboard and say my lesson. I still had much insecurity in my life that I hadn't overcome.

One of the men in front of me, who had been studying in the United States, was sent away because he was not fluent in English. It was my turn to go in. You can probably imagine what I was thinking. It had been a month and a half since I had started learning English and by no means was I fluent in the language. I was paralyzed with fear when two scriptures from the Bible came to my mind. The first one was *"Trust in the Lord with all your heart, and lean not on your own understanding; in all your ways acknowledge Him, and He shall direct your paths."* (Pr. 3:5-6) The second one was from Ps. 37:4 *"Delight yourself in the Lord, and He shall give you the desires of your heart."* I knew that God was with me and my confidence began to come back. My friend continued to encourage me and I was next in line to go in.

Walking through the doors of the consulate, God said to me: "When you go in I want you to testify about me and I will speak through you." I thought, "Now, that is not the best thing to do. How come God always wants to make things more complicated than they already are?" I didn't have much time to argue with God nor did I have any other options. I couldn't rely on my own understanding to answer any of the questions I was about to be asked. When the lady looked at my papers, the first thing that caught her eye was the approval letter from the school. "Victory Bible Institute? Why do you want to go there and why do you believe in God?" Those were two questions requiring the necessary answers from me.

Not only did I find it hard to believe she had just asked me those questions, but I also couldn't believe it when I started speaking in English to her. She was impressed with my English and congratulated me on the fact that I spoke well. I knew that God was really at work in this situation. She continued to talk to me as she looked through my papers. It took five minutes but it seemed like an hour. I was so sure that she would give me a visa, but her answer was not what I expected to hear. My visa was denied that day because I didn't have all the financial papers to prove that I could pay for my schooling.

GOD'S PROMISE IS TESTED

You could probably picture the confusion and the doubts that began to rush to my mind. We got back on the bus to go home, which was three hours away from the capital. It was on that bus ride that I got the revelation that I had to continue to trust God in spite of what I saw happen. If I had a promise, it was going to come to pass even if it wasn't in the timing I had expected. My part was to continue to walk by faith. I went home and told my parents that I didn't get the visa. I had faced 'my red sea' just like Moses and the children of Israel in Exodus 14. It was up to God to part it, but I had to step into the water. I decided that while waiting on God I would continue to rejoice and not allow discouragement to stop me. What else was there to do? My family had to see God at work in my life, and I had no other options but to keep on walking on the water.

After I had gone to bed that night, Mike and Ruth called me from the United States. While praying for me, they had felt to call and see what had happened with my visa. When I woke up the next morning I wasn't sure if I had been dreaming or not. My youth pastors, Bonnie and Randy Downing, were coming back to Bulgaria and Mike and Ruth were going to send the rest of the necessary papers with them. I felt like I didn't have much time to waste and I believed I needed to book a flight to the United States for the following Friday, buy suitcases, pack and tell everyone I was leaving before I even had a visa in my passport.

I wrote that day in my journal, "I am either going to make a fool of myself, or this is really going to happen." Excitement was in my heart. God had begun to part 'my red' sea of impossibilities, I just had to keep on walking. The verses in Isaiah 43:1-2 were used in a song I sung to myself during that weekend.

> *"Fear not, for I have redeemed you. I have called you by your name; You are Mine. When you pass through the waters, I will be with you; and through the rivers, they shall not overflow you. When you walk through the fire, you shall not be burned, nor shall the flame scorch you."*

> Even in the times when our faith is shaken and fear appears more real than God's promise, we are not to be afraid to cry out to Him for help.

God has all the answers and solutions for every situation we face. Even in the times when our faith is shaken and fear appears more real than God's promise, we are not to be afraid to cry out to Him for help. He knows that we'll get scared. He knows that a promise and a miracle won't stop us from doubting Him again. God just wants us to be real with Him.

MY FAITH WAIVERS

As you can see I wasn't totally full of faith, there were many other feelings and thoughts going through my mind, but those are the moments when we have to grab onto that 'Rhema' word and not let it go. God says,

> *"Call to Me, and I will answer you, and show you great and mighty things, which you do not know." (Jer. 33:3)*

The word "call" means, "to call out to someone, cry out, to proclaim, calling someone by name to get their attention." [17] When we call God by name, then He gives us insight into who He is and what He can do. In that particular situation, I called Him – my Helper, my Deliverer, my Provider and He became to me what I needed Him to be. When we cry out to Him for salvation, He becomes our Savior. When we call Him our Healer, He becomes the healing we need. When we call Him our Provider, He becomes the provision. He doesn't give us things. He becomes to us what we call Him. When healing takes place in our body or a provision is made, that is when you receive your revelation. He is not only my Healer and my Provider, but now He has become yours and no one can ever take that away from you.[18]

I continued in my pursuit after God. The next step on my list was to buy suitcases and start packing. I lived in a city of 70,000 people. When my dad and I went shopping we couldn't find any suitcases. It was close to lunch when we finally walked into a shoe store and found one. It was very big and it was made out of dark blue leather. Late that evening, we walked to the other side of town and found one more suitcase which matched the first one. My joke will always be that on that day I bought the only two suitcases there were in my city.

THE PARTING OF A "RED SEA"

"The Lord said to Moses, "Why do you cry to Me? Tell the children of Israel to go forward. 'But lift up your rod, and stretch out your hand over the sea and divide it. And the children of Israel shall go on dry ground through the midst of the sea.'

Then Moses stretched out his hand over the sea; and the Lord caused the sea to go back by a strong east wind all that night, and made the sea into dry land, and the waters were divided. So the children of Israel went into the midst of the sea on the dry ground, and the waters were a wall to them on their right

hand and on their left."
(Ex. 14:15-16; 21-22)

The weekend was gone and it was time for me to go back to the American Consulate. I walked in and I knew that I would get the visa. The lady stamped my papers and asked me to come back at 4:00 pm to pick up my passport with my student visa for the USA. Yes! A 'red sea' was parted and God was faithful to His promise.

While waiting to pick up my passport, Bonnie and Randy took me to buy my airplane ticket, which I had booked the previous week. The computer locked up and the people working there asked us to come back the next day. I needed my ticket that night in order to go back to my hometown. We decided to wait and pray for the computer to start working again. Within the hour it was fixed, so I was getting ready to be booked on a straight flight from Sofia, Bulgaria to New York City, NY.

I had only $500, which was all of my parent's savings. After the fall of the Communist regime, mom was the only one in the family, who continued to work as a teacher. Dad lost his job like many others and could not get reemployed. They loved me very much and in spite of our disagreements about my faith, they still wanted the best for me.

The price for the plane ticket was more than I had expected. According to the Bulgarian regulations you were not allowed to buy a one-way ticket and I was $300 short for the round-trip ticket. What was I going to do? God had it all planned out. He had already asked Bonnie and Randy to help me financially. My heart sunk and I didn't know what to say, when Randy pulled another $300 from his wallet and added it to the rest of the money I had in my hand. God had done exceedingly, abundantly, above all I could have ever dreamed, asked or imagined and I gave Him all the glory. (Eph. 3:20)

THE 'BIG DAY'

On December 5, 1994, my parents took me to the International Airport in Sofia, Bulgaria. It was my 'big day' that I spoke of in chapter one of this book. My parents didn't know what to say to me. We didn't have much time to say "Good-bye" to each other. I had to walk into the check-in area, where only passengers were allowed. I looked back through the glass windows separating my parents and me. Tears were streaming down their cheeks, as they were seeing their only child leaving. Was this young and shy Bulgarian girl going to make it in the land of opportunities and endless choices? I had only a small amount of money to last me for a week and two big, blue suitcases. I had no idea when I would see my family again.

There are times when you feel as though no one cares and you feel forgotten and alone. Some people talk about you and others laugh and criticize you. Always remember that there is One who loves you and believes in you like no other person ever will. There might be times when you don't feel His presence or hear His voice. During these times remind yourself of what Paul said,

> *"Yet in all these things we are more than conquerors through Him who loved us. For I am persuaded that neither death nor life, nor angels nor principalities, nor powers, nor things present nor things to come, nor height nor depth, nor any other created thing, shall be able to separate us from the love of God which is in Christ Jesus our Lord."*
> *(Rom. 8:38-39)*

He was with me on that day and He is with you now as you cross your "Red Sea."

IF YOU HAVE GOD YOU HAVE EVERYTHING

PICTURES

5 months old with my mom & dad
(Slavka and Angel Deminkovi)
1976. Veliko Turnovo. Bulgaria

At my second year Birthday party.
My mom to the left.

18 months old.

the kindergarten wearing
national costume. (First on right)

School program. 6 1/2 years old.
(First on left.)

7 years old
Koslovetz. Bulgaria.

Riding a bicycle.

With Pastor Billy Joe Daugherty
Christmas party. 1996.

With Pastor Sharon Daugherty
Christmas party. 1996.

College Graduation - Victory World Missions
Training Center (1997). Receiving my diploma
from Pastor Billy Joe Daugherty

25 years old.

Ministering at International Gospel
Center in Tulsa, OK (2009).

Ceitci speaking in Tulsa, OK at Victory Christian Center chapel. (2009)

Ministering in Boise, ID (2009).

IF YOU HAVE GOD YOU HAVE EVERYTHING

CHAPTER 6

LOST OR FOUND

The sunlight was making its way through the closed blinds on the window in my room. I was still lying in my bed observing the furniture and the pictures hanging on the wall. There was a knock on the front door of the house. I heard familiar voices. Jim and Stacy Raymond, the pastors of Greater New Life Church in Altoona, KS, whom I had met in Bulgaria earlier that summer, came to Mike and Ruth's home to greet me.

While I was still trying to wake up and figure out where I was, my bed began to shake and I heard rumbling. Our house was near train tracks and every so often a train came through town. I got up to discover my new town and country.

After a long night of flying and driving I was finally in America. It was December 6, 1994, only a few weeks before Christmas. People had already decorated their homes and the smell of Christmas was in the air. This was going to be my first real Christmas in a Christian home. I was excited to find out about the customs and the way this season was celebrated.

I walked to the kitchen and I saw a basket on the counter that was filled with all kinds of fruit. During wintertime in Bulgaria fresh fruits like apples, peaches, pears, etc. were uncommon. Most people would eat canned fruit and vegetables they had prepared during the summer. I saw five or six bananas laying on the side by the basket. They were my favorite and I remembered how my mom used to wait in long lines to buy one or two of them. One time I shared three bananas with my whole family for a week. I would eat a small slice and put it back in the fridge so it would last longer. Now, I had a whole banana and all kinds of other fruits just for me.

CULTURE SHOCK

My shocking experience didn't stop with that. It had actually begun the night before while I was still at the airport. I remember looking at different people rushing through to catch flights. Everything was very different than anything I had ever experienced. The missionaries living in Bulgaria had exposed me to the American culture to some extent, but I still had no idea how I would respond once I was actually in the country. Needless to say, I was in culture shock, which lasted almost a year. Every time you change from a familiar place you will always experience a certain degree of shock. Your body, which could be used to a particular climate, has to readjust to the new one. That was not hard, since it was December. It was cold outside, just like in Bulgaria, with the exception that there was no snow in Kansas.

Actually the hardest thing was for my mind to catch up with what was going on. Many times when we are saturated in a new 'atmosphere,' which includes new ideas, a new life style and new choices, it's very easy for our mind to reject the 'new.' It's not because the 'new thing' is wrong, but it is something our mind is not accustom to and it's safer to think the 'old' way. Changing cultures in the natural is very similar to the renewing of our mind with the Word of God after we become a Christian. When we grow up in a culture of ungodliness and sin, even after being translated into the kingdom of God, and having our spirit cleansed, our mind needs to get reprogrammed. We need to meditate on the things that are noble, just, pure, lovely and of good report (Phil. 4:8). Therefore getting used to the kingdom culture and what God thinks about us takes time, just like it took time for me to get acclimated to the American culture. The key in both of these situations is that no one can do it for you. You have to make the decision to change your thinking.

Shortly after my arrival I realized that if I didn't allow the culture to influence me, I wouldn't be able to influence the culture. Whatever you reject, after a time, will be the same thing that rejects you. I had to find the balance between accepting the new and keeping the old. Not everything in my Bulgarian culture was wrong; it was just different. The 'homework' I imposed upon myself for the next months was to discover what I could use to become better and more effective by combining the good things from both cultures.

> Shortly after my arrival I realized that if I didn't allow the culture to influence me, I wouldn't be able to influence the culture. Whatever you reject, after a time, will be the same thing that rejects you.

"OCEAN OF CHOICES"

I entered into a new season. No matter how many miracles I saw God do in my life, I still had lessons to learn and adjustments I needed to make in my character with God's help. My beginner's class on God's scale began with the first obstacle course, which I call "Ocean of Choices." Was I going to go backwards or forward? America is known as a land of many choices, but making a choice was not something that came natural to me. It took time and effort.

I stared at the big windows, escalators and stores all lit up with Christmas lights. I had found my gate and was waiting to catch the next flight to Kansas City, KS. I could hear the flight attendant announcing something on the speaker, but I couldn't understand what she was saying. Exhaustion was taking over my body. "How can I find out when my flight was leaving?" A group sat right beside me and began speaking in a language more familiar to my ears. They were from Germany and had the same destination. God was still in control! Our flight was delayed for seven hours because of a bad snowstorm in New York, but the German people offered to 'watch over me' while I took a nap.

At last, I arrived in Kansas City, KS, where Mike and Ruth had been waiting for me. It was close to midnight and we still had three hours left to drive to Altoona, KS. I was half awake as I tried to pay attention to the roads and signs on the way. We stopped at a Quick Trip to get gas and something to drink. My eyes popped wide open when I realized that a gas station was open all night. I walked in. Now I was totally awake.

There were all kinds of drinks and snacks that I could pick up myself. I was stunned. Products in most grocery stores in Bulgaria are behind the counter and only the person working there can get it for you. Things have changed now in my country but up to that time I hadn't had an opportunity to pick up what I wanted on my own. There were only two little aisles of food in the store, but I got lost. Perhaps, I was just tired. This will always remain as my favorite memory taken from the first hours I was in America.

After my midnight experience, do you think I could have anything more exciting happen to me? I was being slowly 'broken into the culture." It was only a week before Christmas and we decided to drive over to Tulsa, OK so that I could see my future school and the big city. Tulsa was two hours away from Altoona, KS. Since it was winter, a few snowflakes were flying in the air but not enough to cover the ground. The road was pretty straight and there were no mountains and hills anywhere around. I couldn't believe that you could see so far away without having a mountain to block your view. It was definitely different than my city. As I continued looking in amazement, I saw a house far away from the road surrounded by trees and land for miles. My first question was, "Where are all the neighbors?" Most of the places in Bulgaria and all over Europe are pretty populated and it's very unusual to see only one or two houses on land by itself.

TULSA, OK

I could feel my heart racing from excitement, as we got closer to the big city of Tulsa, OK. We were finally there. The place I saw on post cards and pictures was now real to me. I noticed a few buildings rising up high. That was the way I pictured America to be, with high, tall buildings, with big stores and lights everywhere. At least that is how America appeared when I watched American movies back home. The highways crossing up and down, mixed with many lanes of cars grabbed my attention. Sofia, the capital of Bulgaria and the cities around the Black Sea were the places that had the most traffic. The only traffic I was used to was sheep crossing the two lane roads in the summer when we went to our village to work. Next came the big super-center, Wal-Mart, and of course the mall. My new 'ocean' was getting bigger and deeper. We walked into Wal-Mart and the first place I stopped was the candy and ice cream section. I slowly began walking down each aisle, looking at the different varieties of drinks, food, clothes, material supplies, etc....

The days were over when I would go and get bread without having to think about choosing among ten different kinds. I had to make a decision whether I wanted to eat white bread, wheat bread, corn bread, sliced bread, cheap bread or a little bit more expensive bread. For a person who grew up with all those choices all their life, that was something normal. "But God, what am I going to do? Who is going to choose for me?" To be honest, at that time I was scared to go and shop by myself because I didn't know what to get. I didn't know what I liked or what my favorite foods were. I was starting from "ground zero." When we went to a restaurant I was the last person to order. My mind was still trying to absorb the new information. I was found in Jesus, but I was lost in the stores.

We came back from the mall late that night. I was more worn out from walking in each store, than from the daylong plane flight. I went to bed and began to talk to God in Bulgarian. He was my closest friend, and the only one who spoke and understood my language. Classes were beginning in a month and on the right side of the bed by the nightstand laid the books I had to read. I was starting my first quarter, but it was actually the school's third quarter.

GOD SPEAKS ALL LANGUAGES

As a sense of security I had packed two big "English-Bulgarian/Bulgarian-English" dictionaries. I had ten books to read and having to translate them with dictionaries was not going to speed up the process. I found a nice spot on the bookshelf for both dictionaries and in my mind I told them 'goodbye.' I couldn't lean on my own understanding. God was the one who had asked me to come to the States and now I had to have the full ability to speak the language. It couldn't be a one-time experience while I was in Bulgaria getting my visa. He had given me a promise that also applied for the States. I began to read my books and God began to give me the full understanding of what I was reading. Even if I didn't know the exact meaning of each word I would understand it because of the context of the sentence.

Because of my experience in studying the German language, I was always taught at school that unless you think in the language you are trying to speak you will never be fluent in it. I knew if I had to translate every single word in my mind from Bulgarian into English I would be unsure and very slow to speak. I asked God to give me His wisdom and grace as I was continuing to grow in understanding. Every new word I heard I would put into use and in a few short weeks I was able to think in English while speaking. To this day I don't know how exactly everything happened. What I do know is that I went to school a month later and started taking notes only in English, and I never opened my dictionaries again.

I was beginning to discover more and more that God is all I need. The quote I had read above my friend's couch in Bulgaria was now a real part of my life.

> *"The fear of the Lord is the beginning of wisdom, and the knowledge of the Holy One is understanding."*
> *(Pr. 9:10)*

My new prayer was for God to give me His wisdom, to make me wiser than my actual age. I guess, you could say, I was never afraid to ask God questions, or to tell Him about my needs and desires.

I was 19 yrs old, and I needed to 'grow up' quickly in many areas of my life. "God, how am I going to make it?" Wisdom is knowing the truth and knowing how to

Wisdom is knowing the truth and knowing how to apply it in different situations. Understanding, on the other hand, is the knowledge seasoned and modified by wisdom and insight.

apply it in different situations.[19] Understanding, on the other hand, is the knowledge seasoned and modified by wisdom and insight. The name of Solomon, the author of Proverbs, is associated with the word 'wisdom.' He was called in 1 Kings 4:31 "wiser than all men"[20] because of the simple fact that he knew how to ask for wisdom and apply it when difficulties were at hand. In my search for more of God's truth, wisdom and understanding, I came up to my next lesson. I call it, "God's subject for my personal life."

It was Christmas and many presents were piled up under the tree. We had people over and as I began to unwrap the gifts with my name on them everyone's attention became focused on me. They all wanted to see if I liked what I got. Soon everybody was a little shocked at my reaction, or I should say, no reaction. I didn't know how to express my gratitude and the excitement in my heart. I said, "Thank you," but the joy in my heart was not exactly showing on my face. I was not very expressive of my emotions. I also needed to learn how to receive a compliment, as well as, how to say, "I can do it." You might wonder what I mean by that. Because of my lifestyle under Communism and the insecurities I had during my school years, my self-esteem was very low. That was the next 'giant' I had to overcome; otherwise, I would be in bondage and I would never fully understand God's plan and purpose.

LEARNING TO WALK IN GOD'S FREEDOM

January arrived and I was ready to start school. As I opened the front glass door, my eyes caught a huge world map designed into the floor of the school entrance. Big mirrors across the walls 'paved' the way into the next entrance. Above the mirrors was another map of the world, this time with pictures of people from different nations. While I was intensely looking at the pictures and the flags from different nations, Billy Joe Daugherty (pastor of Victory Christian Center and founder of Victory Bible Institute) walked by me. He shook my hand, looked in my eyes and smiled as he said that they were happy to have me at the school. What seemed as a pretty normal handshake actually became a stepping-stone and a bridge rising above my past.

I had volunteered to work in the school office and one afternoon one of the secretaries complimented my work. I was putting together some information packets, but I didn't think I was doing a good job. A person with no self-esteem or very low self-esteem doesn't know how to accept a compliment. Sometimes that could be accepted as walking in humility. The truth is, it's a false sense of humility because it tries to get the attention back onto the person rejecting the compliment. Not only was I rejecting people's compliments, but I was also rejecting myself and the way God had made me.

God opened my eyes, and I saw through examples set by different people that He was leading me to total freedom in Him. What I love about God is the fact that He loves us too much to leave us the same. If there was a call on my life to minister to people, how could I help anyone else unless I was first made whole? You can be free in an instant, but learning how to walk in the freedom given to you is a process. Jesus told the disciples in John 8:31-36, that we need to know the truth, by abiding in Him and His word, and that the truth will make us free.

"Therefore if the Son makes you free, you shall be free indeed."

I had to apply the truth of what Jesus said about me and exchange it with what I thought about myself. The lid of "I can't do it and I am not good enough" was slowly being lifted off of my mind, as I attended school under the daily influence of God's word. Every time there was a new opportunity to do something I had never done before, instead of rejecting it and disqualifying myself before I even began, my new goal was to accept the challenge and act upon it. I was given many opportunities to practice my decision.

GROWTH AND PAIN

Paul said in Phil. 4:13 *"I can do all things through Christ who strengthens me."*

As I repeated that to myself, I stepped up to the pulpit at the church in Altoona, KS and began to give a five-minute testimony. My voice was quivering and my hands were trembling, but I knew that I had to make the first step and God was going to do the rest. Every person has to go through that process of transformation. If we reject this process, we reject the opportunity to grow and excel. Growing can be painful, but when we allow God to show us the areas in our lives that are still 'under construction,' then He is the one who takes the responsibility and the glory for making them beautiful at the end. The hurts in my heart formed during my school days in Bulgaria were beginning to heal. God believes in His children and He was willing to help me. In that seemingly long, but actually short process of 'changing,' I had to lay down my pride and will and let God do the work. When we try to resist the changes He brings to us, we do harm to ourselves. Somehow or someway, changes will take place, but it might be a longer process; that depends fully on us.

> If we reject this process, we reject the opportunity to grow and excel.

There is a verse in Philippians 3:12 which I have made one of the foundational keys in my life.

> *"I am still not all I should be, but I am bringing all my energies to bear on this one thing: Forgetting the past and looking forward to what lies ahead. I strain to reach the end of the race and receive the prize for which God is calling us up to heaven because of what Christ Jesus did for us." (TLB)*

We will never be perfect, but we can be better. Focusing and pressing might be required, but at the end, what seemed an overbearing obstacle from the past, can now become a stepping-stone for the future.

The day I gave my testimony, when I sat down, a few of my friends turned around and said, "You did awesome." Although I really didn't think so, I decided to smile and say, "Thank you." The more I began to use the words "Thank you" after a compliment, the freer I became on the inside. God restored a new confidence in me, and a new self-esteem that came from knowing Him and His ways.

GOING THROUGH THE NEXT TESTS

By no means were my stretching days over. About a month after school started my right eye developed an infection that caused it to swell. The doctor recommended an operation. In the meantime, one of the fillings in my teeth fell out and I needed to get it fixed. Both things required extra money that I didn't have. It was close to 3:00 am when God woke me up one morning and asked me to pray for different people. I sat in my bed and as I prayed God healed my eye. I didn't know what was taking place until I got up and looked in the mirror. The swelling started to go down. I didn't need surgery any more, only a small shot for protection against new infection. That night God spoke to me and said that when I seek Him first because I love Him and put the needs of others before my own, He would supply everything else that I needed.

> "But seek first the kingdom of God and His righteousness, and all these things shall be added to you." (Matt. 6:33)

NEW MIRACLES

The rest of the provision was on its way. My tooth was fixed for free and my school tuition was paid off right before the 4th quarter began. That month was filled with many miracles. The best one of all was that my God was not only my Savior but also my family's savior. My mom and grandma (my mom's mother) accepted Jesus. There was no distance in prayer, and God had begun a work in my parents' hearts.

There were new 'oceans' to swim and new 'giants' to overcome in the days ahead, but I knew that faithful is He *"...who has begun a good work in us to complete it until the day of Jesus Christ."* (Paraphrased, Phil. 1:6)

CHAPTER 7

KNOWING THE GOD BEHIND THE MIRACLES

It was a late afternoon and the sunset was slowly being painted on the deep blue sky. It looked, as though God had dipped His paintbrush in hot red, orange and bright golden yellow and was gradually portraying a picture of a horizon. I was sitting on the balcony just off of our living room in Tulsa, OK trying to get the most out of the last days of spring. It was already pretty hot, but at least not very humid. I had been warned that summers in Oklahoma are very hot. There was a refreshing breeze that particular night and probably the last one I felt for the rest of the summer. It had been almost six months since I had arrived in the States. I was living at the student housing, and I was waiting to be employed as a nursery worker at the church. The housing in the summer was very quiet. Almost everyone I knew had gone back to visit family and friends. My roommates were working during the day and I had a lot of time to myself.

I remembered what Pastor Billy Joe Daugherty had said in one of our classes, "The vision we have will make us into the person we need to be." I knew in my heart that while I was waiting on a job, I should surround myself with God's vision for my life. How could I continue to change and become better unless God revealed to me the 'spots' that needed to be removed, while waiting in His presence.

GOD STANDS BEHIND THE MIRACLES

I had a new book given to me, called "Good Morning Holy Spirit," by Benny Hinn. As I read it, a hunger began to develop in my heart. I wanted to know the Lord and His Holy Spirit like never before. My heart was craving to be filled with His love and I wanted to be drawn into His arms. It's true that I knew how to hear God's voice. I had seen some of His miracles, but I was not satisfied. Psalm 103:7 says "He made known His ways unto Moses, His acts to the children of Israel." When the children of Israel were in the wilderness, God supernaturally provided manna for them and guided them on the way. They saw the miracles, but didn't know the personality of God. Moses was the one who personally talked to the Lord and had a relationship with Him. (Ex. 33:12-23). When the miracles seemed to cease, the Israelites became disobedient and wanted to return back into their old land. That can happen to us as well. After being a Christian for a while the newness and excitement we feel seems to wear thin. At times the miracles in our life can cease and we naturally desire to go back into our old ways and lifestyle because it is comfortable and predictable.

WHAT HAPPENED TO GOD?

Shortly after finishing Benny Hinn's book, I discovered that before you do anything great for God, He will put you through "His refining fire" to shape your character and expand your heart. The times that seemed so easy to hear from God, all of a sudden had escaped somewhere and the only thing left for me was silence. What happened? How come God left me here? It seemed as though the days had stopped and every minute was expanded into hours.

Even though I couldn't understand all God was doing in my heart, I decided to continue to press in. There was no one else to rely upon but God. My dad had always told me that where there is a will there is a way. Every time something would break at home, he always found a way to fix it. He either asked someone to tell him how to do it, or he would try it himself until it was done. I guess, I decided to take my dad's example and apply it in my personal quest for God's intimate love.

LONGING FOR HIS PRESENCE

One morning as I was reading through Psalms, I came to a familiar chapter.

> *"As the deer pants for the water brooks, so pants my soul for You, O God. My soul thirsts for God, for the living God. When shall I come and appear before God?" (Ps. 42:1-2)*

Tears started streaming down my cheeks. I had a revelation of what the psalmist was talking about. His longing for God's presence had consumed him to such a degree, that the only thing he could compare it with was the way the deer would pant for the waters. The water brooks were a source of life, refreshment and escape.

During hunting season, when the deer is in the water its tracks can no longer be recognized by the hunters. Not only were the waters thirst quenching, but they were also a place of safety. The Holy Spirit began to show me that once we are hidden in God's presence the enemy can't touch us and no one can hurt us because the Lord surrounds us and protects us. I became more aware of what God was doing in me.

In Bulgaria, when I received God's call on my life, I told the Lord that I would preach only those things from His Word that I personally experienced. God knew that if I was to lead people into His presence, I had to know how to get there myself. We can't lead someone into a place we've never been. Song of Solomon 3:3b talks about the bride looking for her bridegroom: *"Have you seen the one I love?"* she asked. He had appeared to her and then He left. The bride is you and I, and the bridegroom is our God. He reveals Himself to us and then He hides, so that we can run after Him and try to find Him. The more we search for Him the more our ego dies. All the pride I had, all my goals and my desires were now being put on the altar with the only purpose of finding the one I loved, and being lost in His presence.

IN HIS PRAYING HANDS

A few days passed and I could tell that suddenly depression and loneliness were beginning to settle in my heart. But why would I feel that way after I had a revelation of what God had for me? In my mind, there

ORU Praying Hands
Tulsa, OK

were so many unanswered questions. Since our housing was right across from Oral Roberts University's campus, every night I could see the two big praying hands all lit up and the nation's banners around them. Our church held the Sunday services in the ORU Mabee Center and our Wednesday night services were held in the building right across the street.

I was having a little pity party after a church service as I was walking back to my apartment. "God, I miss my family and friends, and I am going back to Bulgaria." When we are lonely or depressed, we look at the present conditions through different glasses and therefore it appears difficult to us, but the reality may not be as we think. I stopped walking and turned around to look at the praying hands one more time before I turned at the corner to go into the housing area. My eyes were captured by the vision that appeared before me. I saw myself inside those two praying hands. Right then I heard a voice, so loud and real, as though someone was speaking beside me. "How can you say that no one cares for you, when I am here and I care! You are in the middle of My will, you are in My hands and I am the One that will take care of you. As long as you stay in my will, everything that comes against you will always go around my hands and will never touch you. I will provide for every need you have. You just have to stay hidden in my presence and in my will for your life."

To this day I can remember God's words so clearly. They kept me going and they kept the fear of the unknown from paralyzing my steps. The gifts and callings of God on our lives are irrevocable (Rom. 11:29). If I gave up it would mean that I would have to start everything all over again. God is not sorry for the gifts He has placed in us but when we don't do His will, we will live a miserable life. God in His goodness confirmed His promise to me one more time that night. I went back home and as I was writing it down in my journal, I could feel the presence of God fill my room. The depression and the loneliness were gone. In my pity I hurt God, but yet He still loved me enough to speak to me and to forgive me. I had experienced God's forgiveness when I accepted Him in my heart, but this was the first time I realized how much our sins and disobedience break His heart. After I asked Him to forgive me, I went to bed and woke up the next morning with a new, fresh excitement in me.

IN LOVE WITH GOD

I didn't just love God; I was in love with God. There is a difference. David said in Ps. 27:4,

> *"One thing I have desired of the Lord, that will I seek. That I may dwell in the house of the Lord all the days of my life, to behold the beauty of the Lord and to inquire in His temple."*

When we are in love with God, we continuously think about Him. We are consumed with a desire to please Him and be with Him and to dwell in His presence. David was known as a *"Man after God's heart"* because he knew how to run after the Lord and hide in His presence. He knew how to ask for forgiveness and be transparent before the Lord. Therefore his strength came from knowing the God behind the miracles. God's heart and His desires had become David's heart and desires.

> When we are in love with God, we continuously think about Him. We are consumed with a desire to please Him and be with Him and to dwell in His presence.

Only when hidden in Him, are we able to say together with David:

> *"The Lord is my shepherd; I shall not want. He makes me to lie down in green pastures; He leads me beside the still waters. He restores my soul; He leads me in the paths of righteousness for His name's sake. Yea, though I walk through the valley of the shadow of death, I will fear no evil; for You are with me; Your rod and your staff, they comfort me. You prepare a table before me in the presence of my enemies; You anoint my head with oil; my cup runs over. Surely goodness and mercy shall follow me all the days of my life; and I will dwell in the house of the Lord forever."*

(Ps. 23)

The Holy Spirit continued to work in my heart for the rest of the summer. My prayers had a different focus. It was no longer about what I wanted but it was about what God had for me. I asked the Holy Spirit to help me pray the things that were on God's heart. But how could I know what the heart of God is like?

GETTING TO KNOW THE HEART OF GOD

When we look through the Gospels and read about the disciples, we see that all 12 of them were with Jesus and were taught by Him, but there was something different about John. He was known as "the one, whom Jesus loved." (John 21: 7,20) That is how the other disciples referred to Him. During the night of the last supper, John put his head on Jesus' breast. (John 13:25)[21] The closeness He had with His Savior gave Him the freedom to do that. John was not more special than the rest of the disciples. He just loved His Savior so much that out of that love He took the time to be with Jesus and to get to know the heart of God.

My heart couldn't beat with God's desires unless I was to take the time to lay my head upon His breast and wait in His presence. The rest of the time I had before I started working I spent talking to God and reading His word. It was basically Him and me. I learned how to share with God, my joys, my disappointments, my hopes and my fears and at the same time asking Him to share His heart.

God wants to share His heart with us and it would be foolish for us to think that God's heart doesn't break. It's broken for the people in this world who don't know Him.

God wants to share His heart with us and it would be foolish for us to think that God's heart doesn't break. It's broken for the people in this world who don't know Him. God's brokenness is expressed in His endless love for us, *"that while we were still sinners, Christ died for us."* (Rom. 5:8) The more time I spent with the Lord, the more my heart was broken for the nations. He didn't care only for one country and one person, but I had to hear His heartbeat first before I could help anyone else. The vision for the nations began to grow deeper in me because it was the same as that of my pastor and my church.

Our school classes were held on the east side of Tulsa. The building we were using was given to the church by two powerful evangelists, Dr. T.L. and Daisy Osborn, and it was located right off of a main interstate. During our breaks I would go to the backside of the building where the offices were located and I would look at the pictures on the walls. They were expanded into massive posters capturing crowds of people who had been ministered to by our pastors and also by Dr. T.L. Osborn and his family. I became more and more convinced that preaching and ministering to people was a desire God had placed in my heart, but only He could bring it to pass. I needed more training and practical experience.

WHICH WAY NOW?

At the end of July 1995 I started working at the nursery of the church. The money I saved was still not enough to pay my tuition for the new program I wanted to be in. I had heard of the In Ministry Training (IMT) program that was a part of my school. It was designed for singles from the ages of 19-28. The IMT students attended the Bible School classes in the mornings and had discipleship training in the afternoons. It was going to be 'hands on' experience, and it would train us to preach and minister the Gospel in effective ways. It was exactly what I needed, and I felt in my heart that I should apply.

After paying my bills for the summer and buying books for the next quarter, I didn't have much money left. After my summer experience, I knew that if God had brought me to this point, He would not leave me now. I took another step of faith and went and applied for the IMT program. My new bills now required me to pay $600 each month, which included my tuition and housing rent. I still had to have extra money for personal expenses. Since we had classes all day, outreaches at night and on the weekends, my schedule would not allow me to have time for a job. Would God be able to take care of me? I felt the same assurance in my heart as I felt before I left my country.

When God speaks He means what He says and He never breaks a promise! It doesn't matter how big or how small our needs are, we need to know and believe in the God who stands behind the miracles!

> When God speaks He means what He says and He never breaks a promise! It doesn't matter how big or how small our needs are, we need to know and believe in the God who stands behind the miracles!

"Therefore I say to you, do not worry about your life, what you will eat and what you will drink; nor about your body, what you will put on; Is not life more than food and the body more than clothing? Therefore do not worry about tomorrow, for tomorrow will worry about it's own things. Sufficient for the day is its own trouble." (Matt. 6:25,34)

IF YOU HAVE GOD YOU HAVE EVERYTHING

CHAPTER 8

STANDING IN THE MIDST OF THE FIRE

Sounds of laughter were mixed with a rumbling noise of cars parking and taking off outside the apartments. I could hear someone running up and down the stairs. I walked over to the balcony to see what was going on. People were everywhere, unloading cars and trucks with furniture, boxes of books and baskets of clothes. School was starting in two weeks and new students were moving into housing. The quiet rooms of the apartments were now filled with music, laughter and life. I had moved to a different apartment designated for the In Ministry Training Program students, and I had three new roommates. Everyone was anxious to start the new adventure and learn more about the Lord. Our classes began on Sept. 5th. We had nine months ahead of us for God to lay a firm foundation in our hearts, so that we could stand against the storms once we graduated.

IF YOU HAVE GOD YOU HAVE EVERYTHING

Our morning classes ended around 12:00 pm each day and we had an hour to go home, eat, change clothes and return for our afternoon discipleship classes. Because I was in IMT, I had two directors over me. Ron McIntosh was the VBI director over the school and Bill Meyer was the director of our program.

the Ministry Training Program (IMT). Group picture, 1996.

I still remember our first week when Bill asked us to introduce ourselves. Our group consisted of five girls and nine guys. There was no way we could possibly imagine how much this program was going to affect us. The life-long relationships I built in school during those nine months, and others later in the other program, have caused me to conclude that every person God brings into our lives is of great importance. You are a part of their destiny as much as they are a part of yours. The heart of our leaders, Bill and his wife Leslie, was for us to learn how to love God passionately and to learn how to serve and reach others out of the overflow of the relationship we had with Him.

Evangelism and prayer was the core of the program. For us, evangelism was sharing our best friend, Jesus, with others. Our scripture motto became Daniel 11:32b "the people who know their God, shall be strong, and carry out great exploits." Before we do the exploits, we need to know God. We had calendars for each month and were required to spend at least 30 minutes with the Lord every day.

"STRETCHING DAYS"

I can remember the first week, when we were all sitting in our chairs that were put together in a circle. Bill Meyer came and gave each one of us a rubber band. He stretched it, aimed it towards the whiteboard and let it go. The rubber band hit the word "Destiny" written on the board. Destiny was not something that was going to show up in front of our door one day and greet us, saying, "I am your destiny, would you accept me!" Destiny was a destination God had for us, but we get there by the choices and decisions we make daily. In order for us to hit and fulfill our destiny we had to be stretched and expanded so that we could fly longer and be effective.

By that time I had realized that coming to the States was nothing in comparison to what was ahead of me. Every week we memorized new scriptures, had devotionals in the afternoons, read extra books and served in different departments of our church. Victory Christian Center had close to 10,000 members at that time and offered a lot of learning and volunteer opportunities. One of the best things I discovered during that time was the simple fact that unless you are stretched you don't know how much you can handle and you won't know what you have to offer.

Two weeks into the school year, it was my turn to do a devotional. I was still pretty shy even though God had done a lot of work on my self-esteem. This was going to be my first real mini-message and I wanted to do my best. I used the closet as a preparation place where I could talk to God. I wrote everything that I wanted to say on paper and began to read it out loud. I was not comfortable hearing my own voice. To make it even more practical I went to the mirror and began to preach the message to myself. I had to do that a few times until all the nervousness in me was gone. The only way I could overcome the shyness and become bold was to practice in secret before the Lord.

One of my favorite quotes is by Malcolm Cronk who said, "What isn't won in prayer first, is never won at all." Prayer was not a requirement, but a life source to God. It was in those times when I was in my closet praying and worshiping God that He took the insecurities from me and exchanged them for His abilities to do His will.

Public speaking was not something that was natural for me. October 3, 1995, my director asked me to preach to the youth at Shadow Mountain Hospital. Our group visited there weekly and we would minister to the troubled kids and teens. Now that it was my turn, I had a 15-minute message to prepare. In those days, 15 minutes seemed like 15 hours. What was I going to say? I prepared six pages of notes on the subject "God's Purpose for Your Life." I was being stretched. After worship and a few skits, it was my turn to get up. As I opened my mouth and began to read, God took over. The only thing I could think of was how much those teens needed the Lord and how much He wanted to change their lives. The scriptures and the words were coming out of my mouth and I didn't even have to read every single sentence I wrote down. That night was a continuation of the freeing process God had begun in my heart. It was another opportunity to walk out my freedom. I prayed that my preaching would be mixed with prophetic words and while speaking God would set people free. Just like everything else, we can have many gifts, but we need to learn how to function in them and master them.

BOLDNESS

In our afternoon classes we had the opportunity to pray for each other and if God was speaking something to us, we learned how to recognize if what He was saying was personal or for the whole group. When a prophecy is given to you, it should always be edifying, exhorting and bring confirmation to what God has already been speaking to you. (1 Cor. 14:3) We were always encouraged to practice praying out loud, and if we had a word, to give it and our director would be the one discerning if what was said was from God. The hardest part was stepping out. For me personally, in my beginning stages, God would first show me a picture of what He wanted me to say and my heart would begin to race. That was my queue, to open my mouth and speak out His word! I spoke in obedience and with time it became natural for me to be bold for God.

When Jesus picked His disciples they were only ordinary people who were transformed by the Holy Spirit when He came upon them. Their boldness didn't come from education or theological understanding of the scriptures; it came from hanging out with Jesus. In Acts 3:6-7, Peter and John healed a lame man who was sitting by the gates of the temple begging for money. When the people saw the healing that took place and the boldness that Peter and John had, they marveled and realized that those two had been with Jesus. (Acts 4:13) The only boldness you and I can have, when we stand up to proclaim the Gospel or just share the good news with our friends and relatives, comes only from our 'secret times' with Him. I couldn't release something I didn't have. John and Peter became channels through which God released healing because they had developed a personal relationship with the Lord.

THE IMPOSSIBLE BECOMES POSSIBLE AGAIN

While growing in my ability to better hear God's voice and become bolder when speaking in public, God was also stretching my faith in the realm of finances. October and November were months when God supernaturally provided the money I needed. One time I called the bank and they told me that someone had made a deposit in my account. It seemed like things were going great until December 3rd came and I only had $5 left in my wallet. In two days I was to pay $600 towards my tuition. I called the bank and they told that me that my balance was $10. The amount was not even close to enough. I had a ticket to go back to Bulgaria on the 5th of December; it was a part of my round trip ticket. What was I going to do? God didn't give me a backup plan, He only asked me to come to the United States.

I looked at my finances and my mind said, "You will end up on the street, if you keep on going like this." In my heart I had faith for the impossible. If I didn't pay, I would have to change programs. One thing about God we should all know is that He never starts something without finishing it. That night I gave away the rest of my money and prayed that He would supernaturally provide. What could I lose; I didn't have enough to start with! One of my favorite quotes on giving was, "Behind every penny is a person, behind every nickel is a name and behind every dime is a destiny." (Bill Meyer). Even though $5 was not enough to reach a nation, it was still important and a part of changing lives. If I gave up, what kind of testimony would I have at the end?

I couldn't think of anything else but the fact that my family was watching my life to see what God was doing. My mom told me how she would read my letters when relatives would came over and they would hear about God's goodness and the miracles He performed. It didn't matter that I wasn't there. God was working in their hearts and He was getting them prepared for the time they would accept Him. I wrote in my journal that day, "When God wants to do something beautiful He starts with difficulties, but when He wants to do something more than wonderful, He starts with impossibilities."[22] It was an anonymous quote I had read earlier that day. Underneath it, I added, "God, I've been walking on the water long enough, I am not planning on going back." I knew that God wasn't providing just for me. His provision was also going to serve as a testimony to the fact that with God all things are possible.

WHAT DO I 'SMELL' LIKE?

I went in my closet to pray that night. Clothes were hanging right above my head, but when I closed my eyes it was as though I was in a different world. I could hear a song playing softly on the CD in our apartment. It was Kent Henry singing "You are awesome in this place, mighty God."[23] While sitting in my closet, I could feel the pressure of that 'money mountain' coming over me. God said to me, "I am with you and I will pay your bills on time. You don't have to worry." Then He asked me to read the book of Daniel and particularly chapter 3. It was about three guys, Shadrach, Meshach and Abed-Nego, who believed in God and didn't want to bow before the false 'gods' of king Nebuchadnezzar.[24] The law that the king had given was punishment for everyone who was disobedient. They were thrown in a fiery furnace as a penalty for their decision to not worship the king's 'god,' but the Living God. Daniel 3:24-25, says

> *"Then King Nebuchadnezzar was astonished, and he rose in haste and spoke, saying to his counselors, "Did we not cast three men bound into the midst of the fire?" They answered and said to the king, "True, O King." "Look!" he answered, "I see four men loose, walking in the midst of the fire; and they are not hurt, and the form of the fourth is like the Son of God."*

Because of their decision, Jesus was right there in the midst of their fire and not only was He with them, but the fire had no effect on them. When they took them out, in vs. 27, it says that the hair on their head was not singed and their clothes didn't even smell like fire.

God began to speak to me that problems will always come, but He will be with us in the midst of that problem. The reason they didn't smell like fire was because God's presence surrounded them. When we are in the midst of the problem we can either smell like the problem or we can smell like God's presence. If I kept on talking about my 'financial mountain' I would soon 'smell' like it, but if my focus was to be on Jesus and His presence, then the mountain would no longer seem as big and impossible.

When God shows up in the midst of our fire, He doesn't respond to the need we have for deliverance. He responds to the faith we have in the one who can deliver us. That is why it's important for us to make Him 'our hiding place and shield' (Ps. 119:114a), so that when surrounded by problems or circumstances, our 'clothes' won't be affected. Problems can bring discouragement. When we refocus our eyes and look at the greatness of our God, joy arises within us and becomes our strength.

> When God shows up in the midst of our fire, He doesn't respond to the need we have for deliverance. He responds to the faith we have in the one who can deliver us.

When I came out of my closet I had a 'new smell.' The problem was still there, but I knew God was in the midst of the fire with me.

A MIRACLE IN MOTION

A day passed and I was told that someone had given $200 towards my December tuition. God had already begun the provision. I went to school after the weekend was over and a friend of mine came over and handed me $50 from a family that I didn't know. That same day someone else sent me $50 in the mail and I had $300 all together. I was so excited; I knew God was going to pay my tuition on that same day just as He had promised.

After my class on healing, Pastor Billy Joe Daugherty asked us to go around and pray for people. While standing by my chair looking for someone to pray with, a man walked up to me and asked me if

I had paid my tuition. I told him how God was providing and that I needed $300 before classes were over that day. God had asked him earlier that morning while he was driving to school to pay the rest of my December tuition. He didn't know how much I owed so he had to ask me first. He came back with a check and handed it to me. I almost couldn't believe what was taking place. I ran up to the office with the cash and checks in my hand and paid my bill 30 minutes before classes were over.

GOD'S FAITHFULNESS CONTINUES

God's faithfulness didn't stop there. A week later my IMT director, Bill Meyer, asked me to go see Ron McIntosh, our VBI director. God had told them to give me a scholarship for the rest of the school year. The $600 I had paid for December was given back to me so that I could use it for personal needs. Not only were Shadrach, Meshach and Abed-Nego saved from the fiery furnace, but the king also promoted them. He believed in their God. (Dan. 3:28-30) When we obey the Lord, we are not the only ones who are blessed. There are always people watching our lives. Our obedience to God affects the people around us. I heard it said many times that, "There is always someone waiting on the other side of our obedience." (Tim Storey) If it were not also for the obedience of those God placed in our lives, you and I wouldn't be here today.

It was in those 'hard for my mind to understand' times that God taught me His principles. I will never look at another closet the same way. It was there that I learned how to pray, preach, write and believe. We have to have those 'closet time' experiences with God in order to be strong and do mighty exploits for Him.

The months rolled by quickly and the time came for graduation. By the end of the year we all knew how to give 30 minute sermons, how to witness, how to plan services and most of all how to serve when asked. I was influenced by the lives and the example of the leaders who taught at our school. A fire was ignited in me to see revival spread across America and other nations. Ron McIntosh taught a class called, "Quest for Revival" where we studied the successes and the mistakes of those who had lived before us and had been used by God to do signs and wonders. A flame of fire ignited in us, but it was up to us to keep the flame burning after we graduated.

DREAMS INVOLVE ACTIONS

The last questions Bill Meyer asked us before 'the final day' came were connected with our future. What were our goals, our plans and our dreams?

One particular question grabbed my attention. "What are five things you would not like to do five years from now?" In my answer under #1, I put, 'Sit by the window and only dream about the things I could be doing for God!' It's good to dream, but the dreams we don't act upon only become an illusion in the time to come.

Although I had been stretched in many ways during our IMT program, I felt in my heart to apply at the Victory World Missions Training Center. The school was starting two weeks after graduation and we were going to be trained to work effectively on the Mission field. We would learn about different cultures, types of religions and what the

VWMTC - graduation class.
I'm in front row, second from right.
Carol and Ken East, directors, seated.

greatest hindrances for people on the Mission field were. It was again a mixture of teachings with practical experience. I knew this was a part of God's plan, and He was going to provide for the tuition I needed.

You and I might face 'new fires' in the days ahead, but remember: we are not alone; He is standing in the fire with us!

IF YOU HAVE GOD YOU HAVE EVERYTHING

CHAPTER 9

OBEDIENCE TO GOD IS BETTER THAN A SACRIFICE

The persistent nagging buzz of the alarm clock interrupted my peaceful sleep. I slowly stretched out my arm and turned off the alarm. Still trying to figure out what was happening and where I was, I glanced to see the time. It was 3:45 am, a very early Friday morning of June 7, 1996. Half awake, I got up and looked at the calendar on my desk. It was the weekend our Missions class was going on a survival trip. We were supposed to meet at school by 5:15 am, load the vans and take off by 5:30 am. It was our first weekend of classes and this trip was going to help all of us 'bind together' and learn how to 'survive' the challenges of nature. After traveling a few hours, we came to our campsite. I was excited and in the same time scared. As I looked at the mountain in front of us, I knew it would be my greatest challenge of the weekend. Part of the trip consisted of learning how to work as a team by starting a fire without matches, building a shelter, cooking from scratch, rappelling down a mountain and using a compass as the only source to follow directions to get to a certain destination.

LEARNING NEW THINGS

No one from our group had ever repelled a mountain except the leaders in charge. I curiously looked over the edge of the cliff as one of my friends was making her way down. I had a helmet on my head and a harness around my waist that was connected with a rope that was being pulled and released from those standing on the top of

NWMRC - Rappelling down a cliff
(June 7, 1996)

the mountain. As I made my first step down, the sense of helplessness grabbed me. The rope was the only thing holding me from sliding to the bottom. If I looked down from the height of the mountain, I wouldn't have been able to see where to put my feet. I had to communicate with the person releasing the rope so that they knew when to hold it and when to let it go. The key to rappelling is to relax and allow the rope "to grab" your weight. You then push off the side with your legs using the rope as your main support. Every time I stopped to take a deep breath, everyone watching encouraged and cheered me on. At last, I made it down. Still surprised at myself, I looked up where my friends were clapping and applauding me. You could see beams of excitement on everyone's face as we had achieved the impossible.

My biggest motivation that morning while I was hanging on the rope and wanting to go back up was the shouts of encouragement I could hear, "You are making it! You are almost there!" It reminded me of that scripture in Heb. 12:1-2,

> *"Therefore we also, since we are surrounded by so great a cloud of witnesses, let us lay aside every weight, and the sin which so easily ensnares us, and let us run with endurance the race that is set before us, looking unto Jesus, the author and the finisher of our faith, who for the joy that was set before Him endured the cross, despising the shame, and has sat down at the right hand of the throne of God."*
> *(Heb. 12:1-2)*

STAYING FOCUSED

In all that we do here on the earth, first we have to be sure that what we are doing is for Jesus. He is the author and the finisher of our faith. He is the greatest example we need to follow. You and I were on His mind when He went to the cross. The shame and rejection He endured was not so that He could show us that He is God, but because He loved us. The ones that have lived before us and are now in heaven have left a witness and an example we could follow. If they made it, so can we. Almost every verse of Hebrews chapter 11 starts with the words, "By faith…" It was by faith that Abraham and everyone else after him inherited the promises of God. They had a race to run and a destiny to fulfill, but they had to remain focused on the finish line.

> In all that we do here on the earth, first we have to be sure that what we are doing is for Jesus.

While rappelling I couldn't look in any other direction, just up. When you and I are called by God to do His will, focusing on Jesus is what will keep us from getting sidetracked. When I finally got down the cliff, I couldn't boast in myself, because if the people with the rope had not been in the right place doing the right thing, I would have died. Jesus is that rope that embraces us and holds us, but we have to release our control and go with the flow of His timing.

After the trip was over and we came back to 'civilized' life in the city, the Lord began to show me the next season I was about to enter. I felt in my heart that I was to begin a fulltime ministry, which would consist of traveling and speaking in churches. Because I was in school and worked at the missions school's office to pay for my tuition in the afternoons, the only days I could travel were on the weekends. I was almost 21 years old, and I didn't know a lot of pastors. I couldn't possibly imagine how I could go to different churches since I didn't own a car and didn't have money to buy airplane tickets. My prayer was that if God had called me He would be the one to promote me.

I kept reminding myself of the different ways the Lord had worked in my life, and I decided to start with what I had at the time. Learning how to write and design newsletters was a part of our program and my next goal was to send a newsletter out to the people I knew. I looked at my finances and I had close to $50. It was enough to publish 60 newsletters and mail them out.

STEPPING OUT IN OBEDIENCE

I called Pastor Jim and Stacy Raymond in Altoona, Kansas. I told them that I wanted to preach at their church since I had graduated from my first year of Bible school. Altoona, Kansas, was the first church where I had given my testimony right after I arrived from Bulgaria. It was also the church where I preached my first sermon.

Before I got to Altoona I prayed for God to show me what would happen in the service. I saw a lady being healed from back pain. God said to me that He wanted to perform miracles, but I had to step out in obedience and pray for the people.

Sunday morning came and the church service began. I got up and began to preach. I could feel the anointing of God come over me. I had read many times the scripture in Luke 4:18,

> "The spirit of the Lord is upon Me, because He has anointed Me to preach the Gospel to the poor; He has sent Me to heal the brokenhearted. To proclaim liberty to the captives and recovery of sight to the blind. To set at liberty those who are oppressed, to proclaim the acceptable year of the Lord."

God confirmed many times, while I was praying by myself, that He is the One who anoints us when we spend time in His presence. The anointing basically is God's power flowing through us. His anointing is what breaks yokes and destroys bondages.[25]

When I finished my sermon, God asked me to call out the lady with pain in her back. I could feel my heart pounding and my mind saying, "What if you didn't hear God right? How do you know for sure, if it's Him or not?" Well, to be honest, the only way I could find out was to say it and see what happened. I guess you can say the rest is history. There was a lady and God healed her, as well as everyone else, who needed healing that morning. God backed His word with signs and wonders. I was not the best preacher in the world, nor did I understand every single thing about miracles. What I knew is what I decided to put to practice. God had called me, I preached and it was up to Him to do the rest.

GOD'S ANOINTING WORKS TODAY

Every afternoon after work I went to the school library and watched videos of different evangelists and missionaries who had been used in signs, wonders and miracles. That was one of the best ways for me to learn and be challenged. God continued to expand my faith and hunger to see more of His supernatural power at work. The more I studied about miracles, the more my faith began to grow.

One evening I spent some extra time at the library. Since part of the building was already locked, I decided to walk by Dr. T. L. Osborn's offices. Right before I turned the corner I decided to take a last look at the pictures of the people healed at the crusades he and his family had held. The big smiles and glowing faces were portraying the joy of everyone healed. I was so inspired by those pictures and the videos I had watched that I wanted to pray for someone. A minute later I turned the next corner and I saw a girl I had met earlier that year. She told me that she was really sick and the doctors had recommended that she take the next semester off. Well, I got excited because God told me to lay hands on her and speak healing into her body. I didn't really know what the exact problem was, but I did know what the Lord had told me. It didn't seem like anything happened that day. A few months passed by and I saw her again on our graduation day. She ran up to me and said, "I am graduating today because God healed me when you prayed for me. I didn't have to quit school and the doctor told me not to take any more of my medication."

> The anointing, God's power, is given to us not so that we can boast in the fact that we have it, but for us to use and be a witness for Him.

There are many instances in the Bible, especially in the New Testament where God spoke to the disciples, they obeyed and therefore saw people healed and set free. The anointing, God's power, is given to us not so that we can boast in the fact that we have it, but for us to use and be a witness for Him.

> *"But you shall receive power when the Holy Spirit has come upon you; and you shall be witnesses to Me in Jerusalem, and in all Judea and Samaria and to the end of the earth."*
> *(Acts 1:8)*

After the disciples were filled with the Holy Spirit, they went out ***"And with great power the apostles gave witness to the resurrection of the Lord Jesus. And great grace was upon them all."*** (Acts 4:32) It didn't matter how old, how educated or how much money I had for God to use me. The requirement was to believe that God is able. ***"Jesus is the same yesterday, today and forever"*** (Heb. 13:8) and according to that, if He did it then, He can do it now.

TEETH PROBLEMS?

My summer was going pretty well until one day while eating my lunch I broke a tooth. It was pretty close to the front of my mouth and when I smiled you could see the gap. I went to the dentist, but since I didn't have enough money for a crown he suggested that I let him pull it. He came back with the x-rays and told me that I have developed cavities on the insides of all my teeth. You couldn't see them on the outside, but that was the reason my tooth broke.

During that particular week our church was holding a conference called "Word Explosion." I went to a service that night and when I stood up for praise and worship, I could feel warmth that came over my face and especially my teeth. God was healing me. During the offering time the Lord said to me, "When you release what is in your hand, I will give you what is in mine." I had $70 cash in my wallet. It was not enough to pay for my dental care so I planted it as a seed. Two weeks passed by and nothing happened. One afternoon a man came up to the office and offered to pay for my broken tooth to be fixed as well as any other dental care I needed to have. When I went to the dentist, new x-rays were taken and they showed that there were no cavities in any of my teeth.

During those two weeks of waiting, God had asked me to continue to rejoice and thank Him in advance, not for what had happened, but for the fact that He can turn around all difficulties and afflictions.

> "Rejoice always. Pray without ceasing, in everything give thanks, for this is the will of God in Christ Jesus for you."
> (1 Thess. 5:16-17)

THE REVELATION THAT CHANGED MY LIFE

Now that this 'test' was over, there was an actual school test coming up. As a part of our grade my directors, Ken and Carol East, had asked all of us to write a vision paper. We were to include the vision God had given us with ideas and goals for achievement. After I wrote it down, I took a break with a friend of mine and we went walking around the mall. In my mind I was picturing myself traveling around the world ministering and praying for people. In that 'floating on the clouds' moment, I walked into one of the clothing stores.

The girl working there seemed fairly young. She was pregnant and her face was covered in sadness. The Holy Spirit asked me to go and tell her about the plan Jesus had for her life. My heart began to race, and I knew that this was something I must do. I never liked starting conversations with the question, 'Do you know Jesus?' I was pacing back and forth in the store trying to think about what I needed to say. Nothing came to my mind. I had to do something. Through the window I saw a bookstore right across from us and all of a sudden I had this brilliant idea to go and buy her something. I went and got her a fridge magnet with a little poem on it called, "The footprints." Five minutes later I returned and gave the girl the magnet. God asked me to tell her that the gift I was giving her was from Him and to tell her that He had a plan for her and the child.

Still in shock from what I had just said, she began crying. That day she recommitted her life to the Lord, and the sadness and the depression on her face were replaced with a smile and joy. I walked out of the store feeling as though we had just had a miracle crusade. I was so thrilled about the way God had touched her. In that instant, God spoke something to me that I will never forget, "You will receive the same reward for ministering to this girl as if you had ministered before thousands of other people. The only thing that matters to Me is what you do out of obedience to My voice." God knew the desire in my heart to minister to many, but that would never happen if I didn't learn how to minister to one.

In 1 Samuel 15:22b, the prophet Samuel said to King Saul, *"Behold, to obey is better than a sacrifice."* King Saul didn't fully obey the Lord when he was asked and his half obedience was considered as an act of disobedience. That day the Holy Spirit did something in my heart. It didn't matter how big my vision was, how much I preached or if I ever preached. My actions were out of my love for and obedience to God and not out of trying to fulfill a vision. We must make sure we are in love with God and not just in love with a 'vision' He has for us. The only thing that really matters is doing what He asks of us and not because we see someone else doing it.

DOORS ARE OPENING UP

God opened doors for me to minister and after school was over I began traveling fulltime speaking in churches in the United States. In some services we had only a few people and other times it would be packed. The size of the crowd never bothered me because of the simple truth that God had shown me that day in the mall. Every person matters to God. If He sends me somewhere, I am to obey Him, and He will take care of the rest.

Financial provision continued to come and Greater New Life Church in Altoona, KS became my service agency for the ministry. As God increased my love for the nations, He was moving me into the next season He had prepared.

CREATIVE IDEAS - GOD RESULTS

In April of 1997 I returned to Tulsa, OK after ministering in Seattle, WA for a few months. God laid a burden on my heart to raise money for my relatives and to return back home the following year. My country continued to go through major economical crisis. The exchange rate of the dollar compared to the leva was outrageous. My parent's salary was $80, but the prices in the stores were almost as high as the US. I decided to make T-Shirts and sell them so I could help my family, relatives and friends.

2) years old in Magudia, OR.
Beginning of my ministry.

Back then, the money I got from offerings when I preached was only enough to cover most of my travel expenses and ministry supplies. When I came up with the idea to do T-Shirts, it was going to cost $500 for 250 shirts. While listening to a song "All things are possible" (Hillsongs Australia) God gave me the design for the T-Shirt. I drew a prison wall falling down with the words, *"Praise that brings the victory at your midnight hour."* (Acts 16:25-26) I saw God provide for me, heal me and deliver me, and through it all He taught me how to give Him praise while in the midst of the problems.

That night He spoke to me that the provision was on its way. I had a goal to raise the money before the summer was over and therefore needed to make the T-Shirts right away. A day later, I received a check in the mail for the exact amount needed - $500. God had placed that amount in the heart of Colleen Judd, who sent the check out of obedience to His voice not knowing what I had been praying about. While traveling to churches I was able to sell the T-Shirts and raise $2000 for my family, relatives and friends. It might not seem like much to you, but at that time it was a lot.

To be able to send money to all the people, the individual amounts could not exceed $50. In Luke 9:15-17, before Jesus multiplied the two fish and the five loaves, He asked the disciples to feed the multitudes. When they looked at the thousands of people sitting around, the only thing they could think of was to go and buy more food. When they put what they had into Jesus' hands He multiplied it and it wasn't only enough it was more than enough.

"So they all ate and were filled, and twelve baskets of the leftover fragments were taken up by them." (Luke 9:17)

I prayed that God would multiply each of these gifts of money to everyone who received them. On the bottom of each letter, I wrote: "The money is from God, because He loves you!"

I remembered when missionary groups came to Bulgaria and distributed food. They were Jesus' hands extended in love to us. This was an opportunity for Jesus to touch my family and I was now that source. Another seed of love and faith was planted in the hearts of my relatives. This seed allowed them to see that God loves and cares for them and He wants to meet their needs. Many of them wrote me to tell me how touched they were and how much the money had helped them pay off their bills or buy food, gas, wood and things needed for the winter months. When we release what is in our hands, God is able to take it and multiply it.

MY 'NEW, FAVORITE' MEMORY

In 1998 I returned home for a year. I had an opportunity to see most of my relatives and witness to them about the Lord. Some of them came and heard me preach at the church and others came and saw me at home. I was 22 yrs. old and I was no longer the little shy girl that they remembered. "Is this what America does to a person?" most of them asked in shock. What do you think I said?

With my parents in Veliko Turnovo, Bulgaria. January 2000.

America is a great nation, but it can only influence you to a certain degree and in certain ways. God is the only One who can change us and make us to be more like Him.

My favorite memory from that year was during Christmas. It was Christmas Eve and we were sitting at the table when I heard my parents say, "Let's pray and give God thanks!" After many years of praying for my family, my prayers were answered! My mom, dad and grandma had given their lives to the Lord. We went to church the next morning and my parents sat beside me. There are no words with which I can express the joy I had in my heart. It was our first Christmas together as a family. God had given me a promise, and He was faithful to make it come to pass.

I also had the privilege to lead my grandma (my dad's mom) to the Lord a few months before she passed away. She was lying on the same bed, in the same room where I last saw my grandpa. It was January 2000 and I was back in Bulgaria. This time I knew what to say when grandma asked, 'the hard questions.' All of my relatives had different opportunities to hear about Jesus from me. Some have accepted Him and others are on their way.

CHRISTIAN = WITNESS

When I first got saved and I was still in Bulgaria, I read a verse in Acts 16:31,

> *"Believe on the Lord Jesus Christ and you will be saved, you and your household."*

Paul and Silas were thrown in jail, and after giving praise to the Lord, were supernaturally delivered by Him. When the keeper of the prison saw what had taken place, he wanted to receive Jesus. They told him what to do and verse 32 says, that after they all went to his house, Paul and Silas witnessed to his family and they all believed in God. Paul and Silas were a living testimony of God's existence and power. The only way you and I would be effective in leading others to the Lord is if we have testimonies of God's power working in our lives. James states in James 2:22,

> *"Faith was working together with his (Abraham) works, and by works faith was made perfect."*

He was referring to the fact that faith in God would always produce results in the end. It's not a religious profession, but out of genuine faith and obedience to what God says, we will have testimonies to back up what we believe.[26]

Knowing only the Bible but never seeing God in action in our lives could cause us to become 'religious.' Following only the supernatural but not knowing God's Word, could cause us to be 'weird.'

Knowing only the Bible but never seeing God in action in our lives could cause us to become 'religious.' Following only the supernatural but not knowing God's Word, could cause us to be 'weird.' A balance is brought when we put into practice what we read from the Word and when we allow God to make it a reality in our life. The only thing left for you and me is to obey God when He speaks to us so that promises can be fulfilled and people can be saved! Then everyone will know that we are simply Christians who know their Savior.

CHAPTER 10

CONCLUSION

My heart was racing as I ran through the Dallas, TX airport. I had only a few minutes left to make it to the gate before my flight took off. One more corner left to turn and I would be there. Most of the passengers were already in their seats when I walked on the plane. Sometimes when you are the last person to get on, you have the funny feeling that everyone sitting is staring at you.

I had a window seat located at the back of the plane. Making an effort to slow down my heartbeat, by taking long and deep breaths, I finally sat down. There was a man sitting in the aisle seat next to me occupied with reading his newspaper. I looked through the window but couldn't see much except the wing of the plane.

Just as I was thinking about all the things I had to do when I got back home, God spoke to me to witness to the man beside me.

I looked at him again and sized him up as one of those not so 'talkative' people.

My conversation began with a question everyone asks: "So, where are you flying to?" His response, "I am on a business trip!" indicated that he was not interested in talking. "What should I do?" I thought to myself. "Maybe I should try one more question and see what happens?" You can probably imagine what my next question was. "So, what do you do for a living?" I asked. He smiled and replied he was a teacher. The conversation stopped again. Ok, one more question and I will leave him alone. My mind was searching, trying to think of the appropriate question. With a big smile, I turned again to the man and said, "Well, would you like to know what I do for a living?" Even if he didn't, out of politeness, he answered, "Yes, sure!"

I began telling him a little bit about my life and I told him why I do what I do. During our conversation, he told me how, as a young boy, he had felt God asking him to do the same thing. Many years had passed and he was afraid he had never fully obeyed the Lord. He looked at me again, this time with tears in his eyes and said, 'I don't even serve God any more. I failed, and I never came back to the Lord." God's plan is to restore us and not to condemn us; I needed to share that truth with him. We had an hour to talk and on that flight he recommitted his life back to the Lord. When we arrived in Tulsa, Oklahoma he turned and said to me, "Thank you, for not being afraid to tell me about Jesus! I needed Him!"

FEAR COMES, BUT GOD IS WITH US

I chose to begin this final chapter with this particular story because it reveals that failure or fear of failing can stop us from stepping out and serving God. Peter stepped out of the boat in Matthew 14:29 and began walking on the water towards Jesus. Fear came the moment he looked at the wind and the waves and he began to sink.

> *"Immediately Jesus stretched out His hand and caught him, and said to him, "O you of little faith, why did you doubt?" (Matt. 14:31)*

It was not a question of condemnation to Peter. He was stating the fact, that Peter's faith was underdeveloped. He lacked a certain degree of confidence and trust. If Peter and the rest of the disciples focused only on their mistakes, they would have never become the apostles we read about in the book of Acts.

Failure or fear of failing can stop us from stepping out and serving God.

It's important for us to understand that our faith can grow when we step out on 'the water.' Jesus said,

> *"if you have faith as a mustard seed, you will say to this mountain: Move from here to there, and it will move; and nothing will be impossible for you." (Matt. 17:20)*

We all have that mustard seed of faith in us. When we put it into action, than we begin to exercise it and it starts to grow. The growth of our faith is expressed in the confidence and trust we have in God.[27] The waves of the sea will always be there, but Jesus has the power to calm the storm or walk over the waves.

As you can see the problems that appeared in my life prove that just because God calls us to do something, it may not happen overnight, and it won't be a peaceful ride all the way to the finish line. While getting to our destination we go through different seasons. God teaches us how to recognize the seasons we are in and how to learn from them. That is what strengthens us and makes us grow.

Through the years I have kept a daily journal of what God is speaking or doing in my life. It has helped me to remember where I came from and it gives me focus for where I am going.

DIFFERENT PEOPLE, DIFFERENT CALLINGS

My prayer for you as a reader is to realize that out there 'on the water,' where Jesus is calling your name, is the safest place for us to be. Then He takes care of us and expands our faith to believe. For some people believing and trusting God comes more naturally than for others. You may never have to go through some of the things that I or someone else has had to go through. The reason is because we all have a different destiny. God will only perform the miracles in our life that are in accordance with the call He has for us. The provision and the open doors will follow that call.

> God will only per-
> form the miracles
> in our life that
> are in accordance
> with the call He
> has for us.

What do I mean by that? I have seen many people compare themselves with others. They compare their gifts, their callings, their abilities and their testimonies. Just because someone is not a preacher or a fulltime minister, doesn't mean that they are less important or have a lesser call of God on their life. We are all ministers of the Gospel! We are all called to proclaim His Word! Some of us will do it as a fulltime position, and others while working as managers, teachers, businessmen, engineers, etc.... It's up to God to appoint and it is up to us to accept His calling.

TRUE SUCCESS

True success in God's eyes is not evaluated in accordance to our accomplishments. To Him, true success is doing God's will for our life and being happy while doing it. What 'boat' are you in and where is the 'water' He wants you to walk on? Those are the questions I want to leave you with. You have a different 'sea' than mine, but we have the same God who calms the storms. He picks us up when we fail and offers us many chances to continue to walk on the water with Him. The people, who never step out of their 'boat', remain on the 'shore', or try to escape and handle the 'waves of life' by themselves, will be the ones who become critical and religious. Because they've never been 'wet' by the impossibilities, they cannot understand the joy you and I have after coming out of a storm with our 'clothes still dry.'

In I Samuel 13:14, the Lord spoke to King Saul, through the prophet Samuel saying,

> *"But now your kingdom shall not continue. The Lord has sought for Himself a man after His own heart, and the Lord has commanded him to be commander over His people, because you have not kept what the Lord commanded you."*

David was the next king appointed by God after Saul. The key here was that before David even became a king, God had already spoken of what David would become. He was known as "a man after God's own heart," but God was the one who said it first.

I chose these particular stories to share with you (beginning with my childhood and ending with recent events); to illustrate that God has a plan for our lives. If we are faithful and obedient to Him He will bring it to reality. David's brothers and even his own father (1 Sam. 16, 17) did not see his potential. That did not stop God from using David. Many times people won't see or believe that we can do anything. We have to know that God has spoken to us and hold on to His promise. If I had continued to look at the fact that I was shy, insecure and helpless, I probably wouldn't have left Bulgaria. Be encouraged! Let's take the facts and give them to God and let Him give us His abilities to do His will!

GOD'S PROMISES ALWAYS COME TO PASS

God gave me a word when I was still in Bible school through my director Bill Meyer. I wrote it down and kept it in my heart. God said that one day He would help me write books and use them to change people's lives. It has been six years since that word was spoken, and now it's a reality. There are many more testimonies and miracles that God performed in my life and I will share them in future books. Looking back on my life and seeing how much has taken place in such a short time, I can only say, it's God and He deserves the glory! He has brought many people across my path, which have been like 'parents' to me over the years. I am also grateful for the acquaintances and opportunities to learn 'first hand' from different anointed leaders. He has opened doors and given me opportunities to share His love all across the States as well as other nations."

> Believing and obeying is all that is required for God to use us and do the miraculous in our life!

He is still that same awesome God, who begins the adventure, gives us a purpose for living and calls us to do His will. After we accept the call, He parts our 'red sea' of impossibilities, He finds us even when we get lost in our 'new oceans' and causes us to know the God who stands behind the miracles and who is with us in the midst of the fire. Believing and obeying is all that is required for God to use us and do the miraculous in our life!

Once we have tasted the goodness of God and seen His power in the secret place, we can stand up and proclaim out in the open, until the people of all nations hear, *"If You Have God, You Have Everything!"*

PRAYERS

IF YOU HAVE GOD YOU HAVE EVERYTHING

PRAYER OF SALVATION

Accepting Jesus in your heart is the most important decision you will ever make in your life. It's a choice that will have influence not only on your earthly life, but it will also determine where you spend eternity.

If God has touched your heart, while reading this book and you realize that you have never made Jesus your personal Lord and Savior, now is your opportunity! God can change your life today, the same way He changed mine! He wants to love you and help you!

If you believe that Jesus is the ONLY true God and want Him to come into your heart today, please, read this prayer out loud:

> "Dear Lord Jesus,
> I acknowledge you as the ONLY true God, through whom I can obtain salvation and receive forgiveness. I repent for all of my sins and ask you to forgive me and to cleanse me with your blood. Please, come into my heart and be my Lord and Savior. Fill me with your Holy Spirit and help me to live for you. I chose to serve you and to obey you for the rest of my life! In the Name of Jesus! Amen!"

If you prayed this prayer, I want you to know that now you are no longer alone. Jesus lives in your heart and He will be your best friend. Don't be afraid to call on HIM!

PRAYER OF RESTORATION
AND REDEDICATION

If you have already made Jesus your Lord and Savior, but your heart has grown cold over the years, or you have gone back into your old ways, I want to give you the opportunity to come back to Him today. The only thing you have to do is pray this prayer out loud and mean it in your heart.

The word of God says in Rom. 8:1, *"There is therefore now no condemnation to those who are in Christ Jesus, who do not walk according to the flesh, but according to the Spirit."* It doesn't matter what you have done in the past, there is no sin greater than God's forgiveness and love. He wants to restore your life and heal your broken heart!

> *"Dear Lord Jesus,*
> *I come back to you and ask you to forgive me for all of my sins. I no longer desire to be my own boss, I now ask you to take charge of my life. Restore the years I spent in wandering away from you. Remove the hardness in me and heal my hurting heart. I want to fall in love with you once again, as I was on that day when I first asked you into my heart. I place my life into Your hands and pray that You would use me for Your glory. I choose to serve you for the rest of my life!*
> *I love you Jesus and thank you for loving me back!*
> *In Jesus Name! Amen!"*

> *"If you abide in My word, you are My disciples indeed. And you shall know the truth, and the truth shall make you free."*
> *(John 8:31b-32)*

PRAYER FOR DELIVERANCE FROM OPPRESSION OR DEPRESSION

Over the years I have learned that it doesn't matter how long we have been saved, oppression or depression could still be evident and a part of our lives. I am sure at times we all could get depressed, especially if we are going through hard problems. Some people are constantly depressed and others only during certain occasions. Either way, we need God to help us overcome it!

One of the things I practiced doing when I would find myself slipping into a "depression mode" was simply purpose in my heart to remember something good that God had done in my life and encourage someone else with it. By sharing with others what God has done or how we overcame a particular problem or addiction, we not only encourage them, but we also encourage ourselves. Testifying of a miracle will cause uplifting in our inner man and will bring us back to the truth, that if God did it then, He can do it now!

"Dear Lord Jesus,
I admit that I have a problem with _____, (depression, addiction; you name your problem) and I need your help in overcoming it. I ask that your power would destroy that yoke of bondage in my life and I would be set free in my mind and emotions. I speak for soundness in my mind. I choose to think about your Word and what you have done for me, and not the problems in my life. By the authority I have in Your Name I speak to the spirit of depression and oppression to leave my life and command them to no longer be a part of me. I close the door to any ungodliness and sin and ask you to forgive me. Thank you for setting me free, that I might be a testimony for your glory!
In Jesus Name! Amen!"

IF YOU HAVE GOD YOU HAVE EVERYTHING

ENDNOTES

INTRODUCTION:
1. VBI School Classes 1995-1996
2. Spirit Filled Life Bible Copyright © 1991 by Thomas Nelson, Inc.
   The Holy Bible, New King James Version, Copyright © 1982 by
   Thomas Nelson, Inc.
   Word Wealth Matthew 19:26 "possible" Strong's # 1415

CHAPTER 1: THE ADVENTURE BEGINS
3. Spirit Filled Life Bible Copyright © 1991 by Thomas Nelson, Inc.
   The Holy Bible, New King James Version, Copyright © 1982 by
   Thomas Nelson, Inc.
   Pg. 1055 Commentary for Jeremiah 1:5-12

CHAPTER 2: IN SEARCH OF PURPOSE
4. Spirit Filled Life Bible Copyright © 1991 by Thomas Nelson, Inc.
   1 Thessalonians 5:9-10
5. Spirit Filled Life Bible Copyright © 1991 by Thomas Nelson, Inc
   Kingdom Dynamics, pg. 1902 James 5:13-18
6. Bulgaria_ culture & history
   http://www.goeasteurope.about.com/library/travel/blt_bg5.htm
7. "Bulgaria", Microsoft Encarta - Online Encyclopedia 2002
   http://encarta.msn.com/find/cocise/
   asp?mod=1&ti=0123E000&page=7
   © 1997-2002 Microsoft Corporation.
8. " "
9. " "
10. " "

CHAPTER 3: TIME TO CHOOSE
11. Spirit Filled Life Bible Copyright © 1991 by Thomas Nelson, Inc.
    I Corinthians 1:18,26 Commentary, pg. 1720
12. VBI School Classes 1995-1996

13. Spirit Filled Life Bible Copyright © 1991 by Thomas Nelson, Inc
    Word Wealth for John 15:26 "helper" Strong's # 3875

CHAPTER 4: ACCEPTING GOD'S CALL

14. Pastor Billy Joe Daugherty – WVMTC School Classes, summer of
    1996
15. Spirit Filled Life Bible Copyright © 1991 by Thomas Nelson, Inc.
    "Rhema"/ "Logos" pg. 1408, Matt. 4:4, Word Wealth, Strong's #
    4487
16. Overcoming Faith – VBI classes, 1995-1996

CHAPTER 5: CAN HE PART MY "RED SEA?"

17. Spirit Filled Life Bible Copyright © 1991 by Thomas Nelson, Inc.
    Word Wealth for Jer. 33:3 for the word "call," pg. 1107 Strong's #
    7121
    Kingdom Dynamics for Jer. 33:3, pg. 1108
18. Benny Hinn Daily Program "This Is Your Day"
    Summer of 1997

CHAPTER 6: LOST OR FOUND

19. Spirit Filled Life Bible Copyright © 1991 by Thomas Nelson, Inc.
    Truth in Action through Proverbs, pg. 925
    Truth Section #1
20. Spirit Filled Life Bible Copyright © 1991 by Thomas Nelson, Inc.
    The Book of Proverbs, Author Commentary

CHAPTER 7: KNOWING THE GOD BEHIND THE MIRACLES

21. Spirit Filled Life Bible Copyright © 1991 by Thomas Nelson, Inc.
    John 13:25 commentary, pg. 1601

CHAPTER 8: STANDING IN THE MIDST OF THE FIRE

22. VBI School Classes, Fall 1995
23. © 1993 "You Are Awesome In This Place" - Psalmist Resources/Kent
    Henry Ministries

24. Spirit Filled Life Bible Copyright © 1991 by Thomas Nelson, Inc. Daniel 3:4-7, 19-23 reference

CHAPTER 9: OBEDIENCE IS BETTER THAN A SACRIFICE

25. Pastor Billy Joe Daugherty – VBI; 1995-96
26. Spirit Filled Life Bible Copyright © 1991 by Thomas Nelson, Inc. Pg. 1898, James 2:22, Word Wealth Paraphrased

CHAPTER 10: CONCLUSION

27. Spirit Filled Life Bible Copyright © 1991 by Thomas Nelson, Inc. Spiritual Life, Matt. 17:20, Kingdom Dynamics

ABOUT THE AUTHOR

Ceitci Demirkova was born into Communist Bulgaria on November 6th, 1975 to her parents Slavka and Angel Demirkovi in the city of Veliko Turnovo. There, she grew up as a shy child and experienced severe anxiety and depression as a byproduct of the Communist mindset. In 1989, the Communist government in Bulgaria fell from power, and Ceitci heard the Gospel preached for the first time. At the age of 16, she entered into a personal relationship with Jesus Christ. It was then that God pressed upon her heart that she would one day travel and preach His message to all nations. Thus, after graduating as a German translator from a specialized language high school in Bulgaria, Ceitci set foot in the United States on December 5th, 1994.

The very next month, while still adjusting to a brand new culture and language, Ceitci began her official ministry training at Victory Bible Institute in Tulsa, OK. Not only did God miraculously aid her in overcoming the language barrier, but she also had to directly face her deepest fears, and triumphed! She graduated in May 1996 from the "In Ministry Training Program" at VBI and proceeded to enter the "Victory World Missions Training Program" at Victory Christian Center. She completed her education in the summer of 1997. While still studying, Ceitci threw herself into full-time ministry, and founded the non-profit organization *Ceitci Demirkova Ministries* (July 1996) at the young age of 21. A year later, she was licensed and ordained as a minister by the Greater New Life church, now called Verdigris Valley Christian Center, in Altoona, KS, as well as by Victory Christian Center in Tulsa, OK.

It was in 2005 that Ceitci was able to expand her passion for reaching oppressed children across the world by founding *Changing a Generation*. *Changing a Generation* ministers to both the spiritual and physical needs of children to young adults. Currently, the organization networks with villages, orphanages, and schools in Bulgaria, Ghana, and Uganda. *Changing a Generation* has a mission to improve the lives of these children across the globe through providing meals, schooling, clothing, fresh water, and giving them the love of Jesus…one precious life at a time.

Ceitci also ministers to the body (shape), soul, and spirit of individuals through a health seminar she began in 2007 called *Tri-Sela*. This six-hour seminar aims to help people live a balanced and healthy life. More information can be found at www.tri-sela.org.

In addition to writing *If You Have God, You Have Everything*, Ceitci has published two devotional books called *A Cup of Inspiration, Vol. 1* and *Vol. 2*. These books capture the encouraging thoughts and events from her everyday life. It is that inspiration she's sought to impart into others since beginning ministry. Thus, today she continues to travel across America and the world preaching and teaching, with miracles following in increasing measure. Her purpose for living is to encourage others to dedicate their whole heart to Christ and to discover their value and destiny. With the testimony of deliverance, healing, and overcoming, her message motivates others to look beyond the impossible and directly to Jesus, through whom all things are possible!

If you enjoyed reading
IF YOU HAVE GOD YOU HAVE EVERYTHING,
you'll want to get these other titles by Ceitci Demirkova:

IF YOU HAVE GOD YOU HAVE EVERYTHING: CD

$20.00
This package includes a total of four CDs. The disks capture the voice of Ceitci and she reads aloud to you her book, chapter by chapter.

A CUP OF INSPIRATION - VOL. 1 REVIVING YOUR SOUL IN 21 SIPS

$7.00
Staying true to her inspiring spirit, Ceitci has penned 21 daily devotions for all ages in this book. *A Cup of Inspiration* flows with the refreshing living water of God (the Bible), where each article is like a small sip that will revive your spirit and awaken in you greater passion for Christ.

A CUP OF INSPIRATION - VOL. 2 REVIVING YOUR SOUL IN 21 SIPS

$7.00
Another 21-day devotional book for all ages, straight from the heart and life of Ceitci.

**To order more copies of this book,
please contact:**

In the USA:

Ceitci Demirkova Ministries
PMB 32, 126 SW 148th St. Ste. C-100
Seattle, WA 98166

Tel 206.569.5161
E-mail: info@ceitci.org
Web: www.ceitci.org

In Europe:

Gospel Media
Argongatan 54
703 74 Örebro
Sweden

Tel +46(0)19-186010
Fax +46(0)19-186005
E-mail: info@gospelmedia.se
Web: www.gospelmedia.se

For ministry information write or call:

Ceitci Demirkova Ministries
PMB 32, 126 SW 148th St. Ste. C-100
Seattle, WA 98166
USA

206.569.5161
E-mail: info@ceitci.org
Web: www.ceitci.org

*Please, include your prayer requests
and comments when you write.*